A GUIDE TO INSURABLE INFRASTRUCTURE IN THE PACIFIC

AUGUST 2024

ASIAN DEVELOPMENT BANK

© 2024 Asian Development Bank
6 ADB Avenue, Mandaluyong City, 1550 Metro Manila, Philippines
Tel +63 2 8632 4444; Fax +63 2 8636 2444
www.adb.org

Some rights reserved. Published in 2024.

ISBN 978-92-9270-849-8 (print); 978-92-9270-850-4 (PDF); 978-92-9270-851-1 (ebook)
Publication Stock No. SPR240394-2
DOI: http://dx.doi.org/10.22617/SPR240394-2

Notes:
In this publication, "$" refers to United States dollars unless otherwise stated.
ADB recognizes "China" as the People's Republic of China.

All photos are from ADB unless otherwise indicated.

Cover design by Jake Ruiz.

This guide was prepared by Willis Towers Watson (WTW) and supported by the Asian Development Bank and the World Bank. It also benefited from the support of the Pacific Regional Infrastructure Facility (PRIF) and development partners including the Australian Department of Foreign Affairs and Trade and the New Zealand Ministry of Foreign Affairs and Trade.

Contents

Tables, Figures, and Boxes   iv
Abbreviations   v
Executive Summary   vi

1. Introduction   1

2. Infrastructure Insurance Landscape in the Pacific   3
Region-Specific Risks   3
Insurance Industry in the Pacific   4
Infrastructure Insurance Market in the Pacific   4

3. Insurable Infrastructure Risks   9
Risks Throughout the Life Cycle of Infrastructure Projects   10
Sector-Specific Risks   12

4. Insurance Products for Infrastructure   13
Best Practices for Contractors to Obtain Insurance   13
Insurance Requirements for Infrastructure   15
Insurance Products Available by Country   16

5. Value of Implementing Risk Management and Reduction Measures   19

6. Challenges of Obtaining Insurance Services   22
Overview of Challenges in Obtaining Insurance   22
Risk Management Issues from the Insurers' Perspective   23
Constraints in Insurance Requirements During Procurement   24

7. Recommendations for Improving Access to Insurance During Procurement   26
Risk Management Good Practices   26
Risk Management Advice for Development Partners   27
Sharing Information and Timing   29
Procurement Strategies   31
Recommendations for Government Agencies   33

8. Case for a Pacific Resilient Infrastructure Finance and Insurance Facility   34
Role of a Potential Regional Facility   34
Options for a Facility Platform   36

9. Conclusion   40

Appendixes   42
1   Active Insurance Companies by Country and Their Relevant Product Offerings   42
2   Matching Identified Project Life Cycle Risks with Insurance Products   45
3   Information to B]e Provided to an Insurer at an Early Stage for Contractors' All Risk Policy   48
4   Contractors Operating in the Pacific by Project Value   49
5   People Interviewed, October–December 2023   50

Glossary   51

Tables, Figures, and Boxes

Tables

1	Infrastructure Insurance Market Categorization by Country in the Pacific	6
2	Nature of Risks by Key Infrastructure Life Cycle Stage	10
3	Type of Risks by Infrastructure Life Cycle Stage	11
4	Typical Insurance Policies for Contractors in the Pacific	14
5	Insurance Coverage Requirements from Development Partner Procurement Guidelines	16
6	Main Products Available in the Local Insurance Market per Country	17
7	Risk Management and Reduction Measures Across the Infrastructure Life Cycle	21
8	Example of Climate Risk Management/Reduction Measures in the Energy Sector	21
9	Benefits and Disadvantages of a Regional Facility Approach	39

Figures

1	Life Cycle of Infrastructure Projects	10
2	Considerations for Contractors When Obtaining Insurance for Infrastructure Projects	15
3	Pooling Projects into Diversified Risk Portfolios	36

Boxes

1	Issues in the Pacific that Deter Prospective (Re)Insurers	23
2	Example of Insurance Requirements Set Higher than Obtainable	24

Abbreviations

ADB	Asian Development Bank
DFAT	Australian Department of Foreign Affairs and Trade
FSM	Federated States of Micronesia
IHL	Insurance Holdings Pacific
MFAT	New Zealand Ministry of Foreign Affairs and Trade
PCRIC	Pacific Catastrophe Risk Insurance Company
PNG	Papua New Guinea
PRIF	Pacific Regional Infrastructure Facility
	Note: PRIF partners include ADB, DFAT, MFAT, European Union, European Investment Bank, Japan International Cooperation Agency,, United States Department of State, and the World Bank Group.
RMI	Republic of the Marshall Islands
WTW	Willis Towers Watson

Executive Summary

Resilient infrastructure projects support economic growth, generate jobs, and bolster local incomes. They are crucial to developing countries—in Asia and the Pacific and around the world—as they strive to meet the Sustainable Development Goals and Paris Agreement commitments on climate change. To truly thrive, infrastructure requires the involvement of robust insurance markets to defray the inherent risks in roads, bridges, telecoms, power plants, and the like. Without appropriate insurance, investors may shy away from these ventures, capping economic potential. This guide provides a conceptual framework for obtaining insurance for infrastructure projects in the Pacific in accordance with industry best practices. It aims to improve knowledge and access to insurance within the region.

Pacific Regional Infrastructure Facility (PRIF) partners, which consists of the Asian Development Bank (ADB), Australian Department of Foreign Affairs and Trade, New Zealand Ministry of Foreign Affairs and Trade, European Union, European Investment Bank, Japan International Cooperation Agency, United States Department of State, and the World Bank Group. have a pipeline of projects totaling more than $3.0 billion for 2023–2025, with nine projects topping $100 million, and six between $50 million and $100 million. A healthy insurance sector, involved early in the design stage of infrastructure projects, will get more projects off the ground and bolster economic resilience. It will ensure better project design for sustainable infrastructure built to meet climate and development challenges.

Pacific Insurance Market.
The Pacific countries are often small, far from major markets, and vulnerable to external shocks. They rely heavily on aid and are highly exposed to natural hazards such as tropical cyclones, flooding, drought, volcanic activity, earthquakes, and tsunamis. All of these factors complicate efforts to establish a viable insurance market in the Pacific. National insurance markets in the region lack presence and financial capacity, and contractors struggle to obtain appropriate pricing to insure infrastructure projects.

Insurable risks and corresponding insurance products for infrastructure projects.
Risks in projects, including natural hazards or project delays, can lead to huge losses in time and resources for the (re)insurers, contractors, development partners, and the Pacific governments. These risks can also disrupt implementation and completion of infrastructure projects, meaning the economic and social benefits will not be fully realized. The life cycle of an infrastructure project typically follows six stages with their key associated risks:

- **Initiation.** Cancellation of the project.

- **Planning.** Scope changes and complexity of technical feasibility.

- **Design.** Design errors and omissions, overruns in anticipated time frame.

- **Construction.** Poor safety procedures, accidents, delays, natural hazards.

- **Operation and Maintenance.** Inability to reach desired levels of service.

- **End of Life.** Regulatory issues concerning decommissioning and hazardous waste.

Generally, risk is highest during construction and lowest during planning and design.

Challenges of obtaining insurance.
Contractors have trouble obtaining insurance in part because it is hard to understand what products and services insurers offer, or how to differentiate qualitatively between insurers. Based on the analysis and interviews undertaken for this guide, in many cases smaller contractors are unable to provide the information requested by insurers, leaving insurers unable to consider insurance coverage. Contractors are concerned by the limited time frames in which tenders must be prepared and brokers confirmed that this often leads to unexpectedly high premiums or no offer of insurance coverage at all. Key barriers that Pacific contractors face in obtaining insurance include the following:

- **Insufficient information provided to the insurer**, encouraged by inconsistent and/or piecemeal information requests from insurers.

- **Lack of understanding by project stakeholders of the risks or location**, including lack of suitable risk assessments.

- **Insurance transactions that are too small or on a per project basis**, which don't interest insurers.

To obtain insurance policies, during contract bidding the contractor should do the following:

i. Understand the insurers that operate in the market (including the types of policies they offer, upper limits and deductibles).

ii. Investigate insurance legislation in the country where the works will be conducted (to establish whether they must first seek insurance in the country of works, or whether they can seek it in the international market, with or without requiring an exemption).

iii. Decide whether to approach an insurer directly or through a broker.

iv. Give special consideration to whether obtaining natural hazard insurance is required under the contract, as this is rarely available locally and coverage might need to be placed separately, outside of the contractors' all risk insurance policy, through the international market.

In addition to these steps, it is advised that contractors seek risk engineering surveys early in the design, enforce construction standards, follow building codes, and be willing to take on a larger portion of the risk through a higher deductible or excess.

Risk reduction measures. Risk management including risk reduction measures lower the risks under the direct control of contractors before transferring residual risk to the insurance market, increasing the chances of accessing insurance and potentially reducing premiums. It is also in project stakeholders' interest to ensure enhanced project design by incorporating risk reduction measures for more resilient and impactful investments. Insurers and brokers could also be involved in the definition of risk reduction measures and help quantify the economic cost–benefit of such measures. Following are good practices in risk management for project stakeholders:

- **Quantify the risks**—Quantifying the risks related to infrastructure construction is the first step toward managing them, and the basis for rationally priced insurance by reducing uncertainty and so improving the attractiveness of the project (and the contractor) to (re)insurers.

- **Follow the building code**—Where a national building code exists, complying with the code is seen as a minimum requirement. Baseline national building code requirements are typically improved upon to obtain a more satisfactory design.

- **Use performance-based design**—Expected losses can be significantly reduced for modest initial capital outlay beyond the minimum design standards and help improve risk management.

- **Demonstrate construction quality management**—Contractors demonstrating strong governance, sound organizational culture, health and safety practices, quality assurance, and quality control can demonstrate good risk management.

Good practices for development partners to follow and implement related to risk management include the following:

- **Undertake, or mandate, consistent risk assessments**—This should be undertaken for tropical cyclone and earthquake risks based on project location, to give comfort to underwriters that a proper and consistent risk assessment has been done, with designs reflecting these risks.

- **Develop training programs in risk management**—Provide training in the region to enhance local expertise in risk management, for example to conduct professional on-site risk engineering assessments, health and safety.

- **Consider using SOURCE as a multilateral digital project preparation platform, which consists of ADB, Australian Department of Foreign Affairs and Trade, New Zealand Ministry of Foreign Affairs and Trade, European Union, European Investment Bank, Japan International Cooperation Agency, United States Department of State, and the World Bank Group.**—Promoted by G20, and supported by multilateral development banks, including ADB, African Development Bank, Asian Infrastructure Investment Bank, European Bank for Reconstruction and Development, European Investment Bank, Inter-American Development Bank, Islamic Development Bank, and the World Bank Group. Development partners and project owners should encourage the use of the platform.

Improving access to insurance through information and timing. The following should be done to improve available insurance services and solutions:

- **Project stakeholders, including development partners and contractors, should involve insurance industry brokers and insurance providers early in procurement.** Insurance brokers and companies have a wealth of expertise in construction insurance and are present in most Pacific island countries.

- **Contractors should carefully consider what information the insurance industry requires for each insurance policy type.** They should be aware of the time required to properly collect, create, and present that information.

Improving insurance requirements during procurement. Procurement teams—from development partners and governments—have a major part to play. Many procurement processes are still risk-averse, and many contractors, especially smaller local ones, are unable to obtain appropriate and consistent insurance, given the appetite for risk transfer in the market. This often means local contractors are ineligible for bidding or they are put off from bidding after reviewing the insurance requirements in the conditions of contract. This may leave local contractors unable to take part in the project, to the detriment of the local economy, or mean that the project cannot be implemented. This problem will require reevaluation of development partners' procurement policies. Project stakeholders could consider the following recommendations:

- Project designers should consider carving out disasters triggered by natural hazards risks and obtaining coverage for these risks outside of their general contractors' all-risk insurance policy.

- Project planners should accept longer project timelines to remove the need for key construction during rainy seasons, which can otherwise result in damaged and/or lost materials, and poor build quality. They should calculate adverse weather days allowed in the contract for pausing of work and delayed commencement.

- Government agencies should tailor insurance requirements commensurate with the supply of insurance and the appetite of insurers in the region.

- Development partners can help Pacific governments improve in-country capacity to help contractors better respond to procurement requirements for insurance through capacity building programs.

- Development partners could split contracts into different work sections, based on local contractors' skills and capacities. Smaller contracts may be more feasible for obtaining insurance. Similarly, certain insurable risks could be unbundled.

- Government agencies and development partners could assist local contractors to procure disasters triggered by natural hazards insurance.

There is a tangential, and perhaps greater benefit beyond improved insurance requirements in taking this approach. It contributes to better designed procurement and facilities, more efficient and effective risk reduction and allocation. These considerations will contribute to improved procurement outcomes.

Pooled approach to insurance for infrastructure projects. An international risk pooling insurance facility could be designed to cater to multiple types of infrastructure projects across the pipeline portfolio. Recommendations in this guide for improving procurement may only have their desired impact if they are systematically applied, which can be achieved through a pooled approach. A regional special purpose insurer could be created to offer cover to contractors working on projects where the insurer, capitalized by donor funds, would centrally reinsure excess risk, minimizing insurance costs. Processes could be simplified by the use of standardized policy forms, documentation and, as appropriate, risk modeling. The facility could also seek to leverage the assets of the insurance industry and invite (re)insurers as investors mobilizing private sector financing in infrastructure. Another option would be for development partners or governments to procure insurance for their project portfolio, taking the onus away from contractors and, by benefit of economies of scale, reducing cost.

1 Introduction

The Pacific island countries need to invest heavily in better infrastructure if they are to close significant gaps in electrification, paved roads, ports, telecommunications, sanitation, and so forth. By doing so, governments can provide better essential services, thus reducing poverty and generating the resources to respond to climate change.

Infrastructure is often inadequate and in poor condition in many countries in the Pacific region, due in part to a lack of investment to maintain vital assets. Worse still, natural hazards such as tropical cyclones, earthquakes, and volcanoes often severely damage or destroy the infrastructure that exists, exacerbating the problem.

Numerous development partners, including the Asian Development Bank (ADB) and the World Bank, are providing external support for infrastructure development in the Pacific through financial investment, which require the procurement of goods, works, and services. These investments are helping countries meet the Sustainable Development Goals (SDGs) and the goals of the Paris Agreement agenda on fighting climate change.[1] Ensuring financial flows are consistent with low-emissions and climate-resilient development, the resulting infrastructure is helping countries adapt and support SDG efforts toward climate change.[2]

---

[1] United Nations Framework Convention on Climate Change (UNFCCC). 2024. The Paris Agreement. https://unfccc.int/process-and-meetings/the-paris-agreement; UN. 2024. The 17 Goals. https://sdgs.un.org/goals.

[2] Organisation for Economic Co-operation and Development (OECD). 2018. Climate-Resilient Infrastructure. Policy Perspectives. OECD Environment Policy Paper No. 14. https://www.oecd.org/environment/cc/policy-perspectivesclimate-resilient-infrastructure.pdf.

Private sector financing is also crucial, and the multilateral development banks and other development partners are funding efforts to better tap its vast resources. ADB estimates that external financial support of over $3 billion per year is required to fully address infrastructure needs in the Pacific.[3]

PRIF[4] is a multi-partner coordination and technical assistance facility that is helping with the cause. Established in 2008, it is working to improve the quality and coverage of infrastructure in the region through its interface between development partners[5] and Pacific member countries.[6]

It assists member countries as they develop national infrastructure investment plans, aiming to strengthen planning of credible infrastructure project pipelines and expand their capacities to improve infrastructure. It also helps identify opportunities for private sector participation.

A major barrier to greater investment, is that national contractors in the region (and some international) face significant challenges in obtaining adequate insurance coverage for infrastructure projects. In some cases, such insurance carries higher premiums due to insufficient competition, amid scaled back operations and limited capacity for providing insurance among regional insurance companies. Contractors may thus accept significant risk when insurance for a project is not secured, or worse, fail to implement the project, curtailing economic benefits to the country. Higher insurance costs reduce the pool of contractors that can effectively bid on a project, adding to overall costs. Notably, smaller national contractors may be priced out by high premiums, leaving only mid to large-size contracting companies, who are likely to be based outside of the Pacific island countries, for example in Australia and New Zealand.

PRIF research in 2022–2023[7] found that local and international insurers perceive riskiness in infrastructure projects in the region, due to its remoteness, long delays in completion, regulatory issues, and greater disaster and climate risk exposure.

The situation has been gradually worsening in the last 5 years, with larger insurers reducing their presence in the region, making it difficult to transfer project-related risks, notwithstanding the significance of the Pacific infrastructure project pipeline.

In the short term, this guide provides information to each stakeholder group and recommends ways to widen access to infrastructure projects to small contractors, that is, to help them overcome the barriers to obtain appropriate insurance coverage. When smaller and locally based contractors can compete for projects, it boosts employment, raises capacity among contractors and the local workforce, and produces other benefits and economic multipliers.

Specifically, the guide was developed with an extensive literature review and information gathering through stakeholder interviews with insurers, reinsurers, development partners, governments, and contractors. It supports the broad array of stakeholders in Pacific infrastructure to better understand and navigate the regional insurance market.

The guide provides advice on the insurance landscape in the region (Section 2) and looks into insurable risks for sustainable infrastructure (Section 3). It scrutinizes the available insurance products in the market and key regional insurance providers and summarizes insurance coverage requirements for development partner-funded infrastructure projects (Section 4). It also advises on risk reduction options (Section 5) and outlines challenges for obtaining insurance services (Section 6). In procurement, it aims to ensure that insurance requirements in bidding documents and contracts are appropriate and proportional to the associated risks of the specific infrastructure project and neither limit competition nor hinder contractors' profitability (Section 7).

In the medium to longer terms, the guide discusses other solutions such as a regional facility which could be designed and implemented to improve access to insurance for contractors (Section 8).

---

3   PRIF. Enhancing Procurement Practice and Local Content in Pacific Infrastructure. https://www.theprif.org/sites/ default/files/documents/Enhancing%20Procurement%20Practice%20and%20Local%20Content%20in%20Pacific%20 Infrastructure_WEB_0.pdf.

4   PRIF. https://theprif.org/.

5   PRIF donors include ADB, Australian Department of Foreign Affairs and Trade, European Union, European Investment Bank, Japan International Cooperation Agency, New Zealand Ministry for Foreign Affairs and Trade, United States Department of State, and the World Bank Group.

6   Member countries include the Cook Islands, the Federated States of Micronesia, Fiji, Kiribati, Nauru, Niue, Palau, the Republic of the Marshall Islands, Samoa, Solomon Islands, Tonga, Tuvalu, and Vanuatu. Papua New Guinea (PNG) is an associate member.

7   PRIF. 2024. Insurance Risk Management and Insurance in the Pacific. Consultant's Report. Sydney. https://thepriforg/document/regional/infrastructure-insurance/insurance-risk-management-and-insurance-pacific.

2

Infrastructure Insurance Landscape in the Pacific

This section reviews the specific risks that Pacific countries face and that hinder contractors as they seek to obtain adequate insurance for infrastructure projects. It reviews the main (re)insurance companies and brokers operating in the region and analyzes the insurance landscape.

PRIF partners have identified roughly $3.2 billion worth of infrastructure projects in their pipeline in the Pacific island countries throughout 2023–2025. Nine projects are over $100 million, of which six are in the transport sector and three in the energy sector; seven projects come in between $50 million and $100 million, five in the transport sector and two in the energy sector. The majority are below $50 million, and 33 projects each have a value of less than $5 million. The average project value is $36 million. The exact period over which this investment will occur may vary and the PRIF project pipeline is only a portion of overall infrastructure investment in the Pacific countries.

Region-Specific Risks

The Pacific countries are small, far from major markets, and vulnerable to external shocks. Small island states are the most vulnerable to climate change. Located in part around the Pacific Ring of Fire, a tectonic belt running around the Pacific Ocean, many of them are extremely vulnerable to geological risks such as earthquakes, tsunamis, and volcanic eruptions. Tropical cyclones, floods, and droughts loom in most of them.

Most of the countries have small economies and rely heavily on outside financial aid, which constitutes over

20% of gross domestic product in Kiribati, Niue, Nauru, Tonga, and Tuvalu.[8] Financial capacity is limited, and domestic insurance markets are relatively small and undeveloped, with limited access to international insurance markets. These factors make it more difficult for contractors to obtain appropriate pricing on insurance for the Pacific's pipeline of projects.

Indeed, the general view of the Pacific insurance landscape—based on consultations with insurers, brokers, and development agencies—is that it is relatively undeveloped. Its insurance offerings are seen as limited due to the very few operators in the region, worsened by the low appetite of the region's insurers to take on significant risk. From an insurer's perspective, high exposure to natural hazards and previous losses from disasters triggered by natural hazards are significant risks, along with the perceived poor-quality design and construction of buildings and infrastructure. Available insurance coverage often falls short of insurance levels required for infrastructure projects. For example, a medium-sized contractor stated that, typically, such projects could require a public liability limit of ~$13 million,[9] yet domestic insurance companies might not be able to offer more than $2 million. One might deem these insurance requirements too high for local market offerings.

Multiple stakeholders have also highlighted country-specific legislation and regulations related to insurance as a hindrance to obtaining insurance for infrastructure projects, partly due to varying regulations in each country, which require time and effort to understand prior to obtaining insurance. The following subsections summarize insights and views from contractors, insurers, and brokers on the insurance market landscape in the Pacific region.

Insurance Industry in the Pacific
Three main regional insurance players have recently offered insurance policies for infrastructure projects in the Pacific, although they do not necessarily operate in every country: Tower Insurance, Capital Insurance, and QBE Pacific. Additionally, in Fiji, New India Assurance, a Government of India state-owned insurance company, has been identified as an active market participant for infrastructure insurance.

Insurers in the region say the insurance market has little appetite for infrastructure and construction in the Pacific. In their view the market is relatively small, with poor loss records and numerous events causing damage and losses, with high risk and low premium accumulation driving a belief that capital can be better deployed elsewhere. Although these three main insurers remain present, they have downscaled significantly in recent years. QBE Pacific recently sold its operations in Papua New Guinea (PNG), and Alpha Insurance has now taken over the previous QBE Pacific operations and Tower Insurance operations in PNG. One reason for this downscaling is that past losses exceed the sum of paid premiums to insurers in the region, making continued participation hard to justify to management.

In addition to the three largest regional insurers, most of the Pacific countries with regulated markets have smaller domestic insurance companies, with typically limited financial capacity to engage in construction-related insurance, such as Fiji-based companies Sun Insurance and FijiCare. Access to insurance typically increases with the size of the economy, as larger economies tend to have more developed financial markets, more market players, and a greater volume of insurance transactions.

Pacific Reinsurance Ltd. is the only known national reinsurer in the Pacific, domiciled in Port Moresby, PNG. International reinsurance companies operating in the Pacific include companies such as Swiss Re, Munich Re, Trans Re, Hannover Re, and R+V.

Several regional brokers cover one or more countries, such as IHL (Fiji) or Kanda (PNG). Additionally, international insurance brokers operate in the region, including WTW, Aon, Marsh, and Lockton. The larger international brokers have licenses to operate directly in some Pacific countries, for example, WTW New Zealand in Samoa and the Cook Islands. They may also partner with national third-party brokers if they do not have a license to operate directly in that country. If WTW wants to do business in Fiji, for example, it must operate through IHL, based on its partnership with IHL.

Infrastructure Insurance Market in the Pacific
Recently published data on the construction insurance sector in the Pacific showed that 2020 was a pivotal year, not only due to the coronavirus disease (COVID-19), but also major disasters due to natural hazards. In 2020, insurers considered coverage

---

[8] V. Ramachandran and J. S. Masood. 2019. Are the Pacific Islands Insurable? Challenges and Opportunities for Disaster Risk Finance. Centre for Global Development Working Paper 516. https://www.cgdev.org/sites/default/files/WP516-Ramachandran-Are-The-Pacific-Islands-Insurable_0.pdf.

[9] Converted from A$20 million using exchange rate A$1 = $0.65 on 5 February 2024. https://www.oanda.com/currencyconverter/en/?from=AUD&to=USD&amount=1.

A Guide to Insurable Infrastructure in the Pacific

restrictions on all new insurance placements in the construction sector.[10] Market capacity decreased, and insurance pricing increased overall in the Pacific market. Average insurance premium rates in the contract works insurance market increased 30%–35%, in 2020 from 2019, after insurers exited the Pacific market. Average premium rates for construction third-party liability increased 15% in 2020 and professional indemnity premium increases were substantial. These factors made obtaining insurance for natural hazard exposure exceedingly difficult (likewise for other project-related risks). In 2021, insurers continued to reduce their exposure by reducing insurance issued in the contract works market, leading to premium increases of up to 25% during 2020 and 2021. Additionally, insurers identified water damage as a key concern, with extensive claims in this area leading to premium increases, sub-limits in contracts, or exclusions for water damage altogether.

The construction liability market acknowledged the same trends, with a 15% increase in average premium cost in 2021 for primary layer insurance contracts (policies that cover more frequent small to medium, high frequency losses).[11] Contractors also confirmed these general trends in the infrastructure insurance industry. One contractor noted that premium rates rose from 0.5%–1% of the contract value in 2015 to 1.8%–2.5% in 2023, increasing up to 3% in places such as PNG. Additionally, a medium-sized contractor noted that since 2016 its general policy deductible

had increased from $10,000 to $50,000 in 2021, with natural hazard minimum deductibles increasing from $10,000 in 2016 to $250,000 in 2021. Another medium-sized contracting firm noted that if it managed to secure cyclone insurance, this would add an extra 50% to base premium costs.

Contractors find it easier to obtain insurance for the Pacific island projects in developed markets with several operating insurers (for example, Fiji and PNG) than less developed or less established markets (for example, Palau).

No "one market fits all" in the Pacific—they vary considerably. Contractors have trouble accessing adequate insurance not only because insurance offerings are lacking, but also because insurance legislation and regulation differ in each country. In general, the region can be broken into three main subregions from an insurance market perspective, related to the level of established market players, competition, and regulation (Table 1).

(Re)insurers assess contractors as part of the risk and hence it is important to understand the landscape they are operating in. Appendix 4 looks at contractors operating in the Pacific countries, split into three categories based on the approximate project value in US dollars. When first seeking coverage for infrastructure projects, contractors in the region typically approach a broker who can help source insurance

[10] Marsh. 2021. Construction Insurance Market Recap 2020. https://www.marsh.com/au/industries/construction/insights/construction-insurance-market-recap-2020.html.

[11] Marsh. 2022. Construction 2021 Pacific Insurance Market Recap. https://www.marsh.com/au/industries/construction/insights/construction-2021-pacific-insurance-market-recap-report.html.

Table 1. Infrastructure Insurance Market Categorization by Country in the Pacific

Pacific Subregion	Countries	Insurance Availability for Construction Projects	PRIF Project Pipeline (approximate % share of project value)
Established markets with a strong construction insurance presence	• PNG • Fiji • Solomon Islands • Vanuatu	Strong lead insurers are present, such as QBE Pacific, Tower Insurance, and Capital Insurance. Established construction insurance markets exist. QBE Pacific is a market leader in construction insurance domiciled in each of these countries, apart from PNG, where Alpha recently bought QBE's Pacific PNG operations. The insurance markets in these countries have regulations in place.	~70
Established markets without a strong construction insurance presence	• Cook Islands • Tonga • Samoa	Limited lead insurers present. These markets have established participants like Tower, Federal insurance, and Capital but these firms lack strong construction insurance capability or capacity to support larger projects. These insurance markets have regulations in place.	~20
Less established or unregulated markets	• FSM • Kiribati • Nauru • Niue • Palau • RMI • Tuvalu	No lead insurers present in country, local insurance provision is limited, as is regulations, and coverage for construction insurance is reliant on overseas insurers.	~10

PRIF = Pacific Regional Infrastructure Facility   PNG=Papua New Guinea
FSM= Federated States of Micronesia   RMI= Republic of the Marshall Islands

Source: WTW.

cover from local or international insurance providers or through co-insurance (more than one insurer).

Those countries without a local insurance market, such as Tuvalu and Nauru, can be assisted by international or regional brokers. For example, a broker who is part of "complete insurance services" based in Fiji will place insurance with New India Assurance in Fiji. This is on a case-by-case basis, and not on the scale of Pacific infrastructure projects, but has been known to provide fishing and manufacturing insurance, as well as insurance for oil tankers.

QBE Pacific is perceived to be well-positioned to offer cover for more complex risks, said a large broker operating in Australia, so it could be considered when seeking cover for infrastructure projects. However, the firm is still known to be stringent on what cover it provides and typically will only insure parts of a project. Additionally, QBE Pacific is seen to be well-placed to offer natural hazard insurance, whereas local insurers will either not cover it or cover it at unaffordable premiums. Further, some insurance markets, for example in Fiji, cannot cover tropical cyclone risk for infrastructure projects, as insurers require an engineering certificate authorized by the Fiji Council of the institute Engineers Fiji, which is provided only for completed buildings or infrastructure, so by nature will not be available if a project is in the construction phase. Beyond QBE Pacific and Tower, it is hard to obtain additional providers in the region for insurance,

especially for disasters triggered by natural hazards risk. The lack of insurance providers is mainly because of the direct and indirect costs of insuring one project at a time, the lack of a diversified portfolio of different types of risks, and insufficient business to build up enough reserves from premium payments to pay claims for extreme but plausible events in the region, such as tropical cyclones. One single claim can easily exceed the accumulated premium for the country or the region, leading to unwelcome volatility and/or relatively expensive reinsurance, reducing profitability.

Local market appetite for complex projects such as dams, water projects, bridges, and roads is also minimal, said one local insurer, as such projects use expensive niche equipment during construction that has significant risk of catching fire, which would consume the entire premium pool in claims. Lower value projects, ranging between $1 million and $5 million, are more likely to find insurance from local insurers.

The largest single risk for infrastructure projects in the Pacific, said another local insurer, is delay in construction and commissioning, sapping insurer appetite for business interruption insurance. Rather, local insurers prefer "non-complex" projects—simple and small structures such as schools, evacuation centers, and village halls, below three stories. Even with simpler projects, however, cover will typically be limited to fire and theft; tropical cyclone cover will be lacking, as loose materials are at high risk from cyclone winds.

In the Pacific countries, loss adjusters, valuers, and risk engineers are also lacking, yet required for a functional indemnity insurance industry. This likewise creates challenges of providing insurance coverage and getting claims settled.

If brokers can find a local insurer able to cover the risk, they will try to work with them, but if they offer insufficient capacity and/or partial coverage, they will look at co-insurance. For example, one broker noted that in 2022–2023, it had placed cover for its clients with the following splits: 25%–50% with a local insurer and 50%–75% with the international markets (Australia, London, or Singapore). Accessing the international insurance market faces obstacles, including legislative barriers such as having to prove coverage cannot be obtained in-country. International insurance markets may prefer larger or more established contractors and require premium levels and/or policy terms outside the appetite of local contractors.

Among international markets, London plays a major role: for example, W/R/B and Lloyd's will insure some Pacific risks. Major firms not based in London such as Trans Re, Hannover Re, R+V, Swiss Re, and Munich Re will too. However, their appetite is selective, and whether they decide to insure a project will depend on the nature and characteristics of that project and its location.

Countries with more developed insurance market regulations require an exemption to allow international insurers to operate in their country and to support the protection and development of local insurance markets. For example, Fiji, Solomon Islands, and Vanuatu are legally required to use local insurance companies where cover is available. However, in countries where the local regulator has little capacity, it can be a challenging and lengthy process to get regulatory clearance. This limits providers and drives up prices; contractors may not be able to access other insurance markets in time. Countries such as Nauru and Niue, which do not have an active insurance market, do not have insurance-related legislation, so a license is not needed for international brokers or insurers to operate there. In this case, firms operating in these countries face less regulatory restriction to access international brokers and insurance services. However, insurer appetite for insuring projects in these countries can still be limited, given the small geographic concentration of risks, the lack of local technical support services such as engineers and loss adjusters, and insufficient knowledge of local regulatory or political risks.

While local suppliers and contractors tend to insure on a per project basis, larger international contractors have an advantage in that they buy company-wide insurance centrally, with each new projects added upon award.

Local contractors that usually work on government-funded projects are often not required by their government to buy insurance for these projects, such as liability insurance. Hence, understanding of insurance by local contractors can be lacking, which can constrain their efforts to obtain insurance for donor-funded projects. In smaller Pacific countries, construction sector professional services—such as risk engineering, quality assurance, loss assessment, and adjustment and regulatory support—are poor or nonexistent, making it challenging for local contractors to implement small projects.

Declining insurer capacity is not unique to the Pacific island countries. In Australia, capacity in the construction insurance market also declined, pushing premiums up to 10% higher in the first half of 2023,[12] compared to the previous year. Similarly, WTW's Global Construction Rate Trend Report (2023) says limits have declined globally, especially for construction projects exposed to natural hazard risks.[13] If premiums and deductibles are increasing in developed economies and limits decreasing, then this problem is even worse for developing countries, where smaller insurance companies operate, and risks are more volatile.

[12]   Interview with Maarten van Haaps. 2023. Marsh. LinkedIn interview.

[13]   WTW. 2023. Global Construction Rate Trend Report. https://www.wtwco.com/en-sg/insights/2023/09/global-construction-rate-trend-report#:~:text=According%20to%20Global%20Data%2C%20overall,annual%20average%20rate%20of%206.4%25.

A Guide to Insurable Infrastructure in the Pacific

3

Insurable Infrastructure Risks

nfrastructure development is critical to economic growth, generating many job opportunities and bolstering local income. Several paramount risks associated with the project life cycles of infrastructure projects can nonetheless lead to huge losses in time and resources for those that bear the risks, including (re)insurers, contractors, financiers, and development partners.[14] These risks can disrupt the completion of infrastructure projects, meaning that the full economic and social benefits of the projects may not be realized. If these risks are not well managed, mitigated, or transferred, they may also affect the investment pipeline.

Construction projects hold many risks, and it is difficult to determine the impact of each variable independently, due to difficulties in calculating each factor's dependence and correlation with other risk factors. From the perspective of multiple insurers, the Pacific construction industry has a reputation for poor risk management, a perception exacerbated in countries where the workforce is less qualified to implement risk management strategies. To successfully manage the project risks, they must be identified, quantified, and managed through risk reduction, with residual risk transferred via insurance.

This section defines the key stages in the life cycle of an infrastructure project and the nature of the risks present at each stage. Specific risks (insurable and non-insurable "business" risks) at each stage of the life cycle are identified and it concludes with sector-specific risks.

14   S. M. Renuka, C. Umarani, and S. Kamal. 2014. A Review on Critical Risk Factors in the Life Cycle of Construction Projects. *Journal of Civil Engineering Research.* 4(2A): pp. 31–36. https://www.researchgate.net/profile/Kamal-Selvaraj-2/publication/288007778_A_review_on_critical_risk_ftors_in_the_life_cycle_of_construction_projects/links/5c89b399a6fdcc3817526d49/A-review-on-critical-risk-factors-in-the-life-cycle-of-construction-projects.pdf.

Risks Throughout the Life Cycle of Infrastructure Projects

While development partners have different sector groupings, within PRIF's consolidated development partner pipeline, infrastructure projects fall into sectors, defined as: transport, energy, water and sanitation, urban development, and information and communication technology (ICT). Despite the broad scope of project sectors, the life cycle of an infrastructure project will generally follow the format shown in Figure 1.

Each stage of an infrastructure project carries different types of risk and therefore different required levels of risk management and risk transfer. In general, risk is considered highest in the construction phase and lowest in the planning and design phases. However, the risks for each stage should be identified and managed in the planning and design phase. Table 2 presents the nature of risks by key project stage.

Figure 1. Life Cycle of Infrastructure Projects

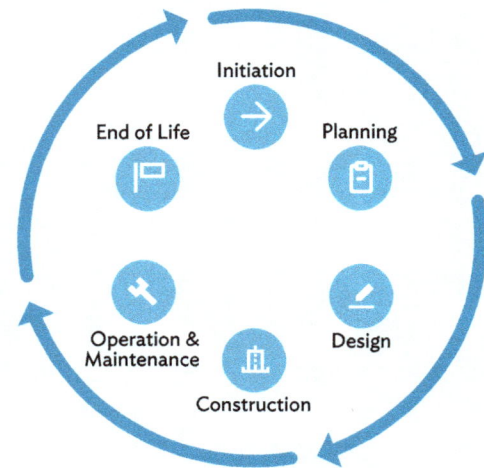

Source: WTW.

Table 2. Nature of Risks by Key Infrastructure Life Cycle Stage

Life Cycle	Definition	Nature of Risk
Planning and Design	Creating the objectives, description, and design features of a new infrastructure project, including the identification of activities and resources required to execute this project.	Risks are relatively lower at this stage before the start of physical work. Risks to project owners are largely the investment made during this phase, which is often borne directly by the investors without insurance or other risk transfers. Risks to the professionals involved are mostly of two types: (i) nonpayment by owner, particularly if the project fails at this stage, and (ii) professional liability for errors and omissions. However, in the context of the Pacific countries, risks for designers are particularly exacerbated by building codes (e.g., outdated, missing, or poorly designed building codes), and compliance during construction (e.g., unenforced building codes and lack of engineers to audit compliance to design and code).
Construction	Implementing and building the project that was undetaken in the planning and design stage.	The construction stage of infrastructure projects has the greatest risk, particularly physical risk such as accidents, and business interruption and/or project delays, which are largely borne by the construction contractor. Further to this, external risks and natural hazards, such as those posed by tropical cyclones, are highest at this stage due to loose materials being extremely vulnerable to high winds, or perishable materials being vulnerable to flooding that often accompany cyclones in the Pacific. A local insurer in Fiji noted that construction delays are perceived as the biggest risk to infrastructure projects. Insurers often do not want to get involved, especially if there are some performance indicators built into the contract, for example a statement that the completion of construction must be achieved by a specified date. This can make the project uninsurable for local contractors, while large contractors can access project delays insurance through the international market.
Operation and Maintenance	Functions, duties, labor, and resources associated with the daily operations and upkeep of the infrastructure asset during its lifespan.	Pacific country governments in this guide rarely have sufficient technical capacity to manage and implement maintenance plans or sufficient funding and/or budget allocation to finance maintenance when it is required after an infrastructure project is complete.[a] This can shorten the life of the infrastructure asset, requiring major rehabilitation or rebuilding earlier than envisaged. The cost to maintain infrastructure in the Pacific countries has been estimated as equivalent to 6% of their gross domestic product. Although contractors will usually not bear this risk, it is important that project owners execute adequate planning and expertise for maintaining newly built structures if they would like to obtain insurance to manage this risk.

[a] Economic and Social Commission for Asia and the Pacific, Pacific Office. 2015. Financing for Development: Infrastructure Development in the Pacific Islands. *MPDD Working Paper.* WP/15/02. https://www.unescap.org/sites/default/files/2-ESCAP-Infrastructure%20Financing%20Pacific-July2015_share_2.pdf.

Source: WTW.

Table 3 looks at key specific risks for the different stages of an infrastructure project (not an exhaustive list of risks).[15] These risks can cause disruption and losses and therefore must be managed and mitigated where possible in the first instance.

Table 3. Type of Risks by Infrastructure Life Cycle Stage

Life Cycle Stage	Risks	
Initiation	Cancellation of project	
Planning	Scope and design changes	
	Scheduling errors, contractor delays	
	Cost overrun	
	Loss of paperwork (e.g., contract by theft, carelessness, or misplacement)	
	Technical feasibility	
	Economic viability	
	Inadequate scope of work	
	Project complexity	
	Material provision (sole source/or service providers)	
	Inadequate selection of contract types (e.g., lump sum, unit price, cost plus, etc.)	
Design	Design errors and omissions	Loss of paperwork
	Overruns anticipated timeframe	Inaccurate data
	Late changes requested by stakeholders	Nonpayment by owner
	Non-abidance of the design contract	
Construction	Property cost overruns	Wage scales
	Technology changes	Delays (e.g., in possession of site, design and/or drawings, materials, completion)
	Inflation	Problem with site conditions (e.g., soil, utilities)
	Inadequate managerial skills, improper coordination between teams	Noise, fumes, and dust
	Poor safety procedures and/or accidents	Hazardous waste
	Injury to public and/or workers	Defective materials
	Natural hazards	Delays in designs and drawings
	Inexperienced workforce	Errors in designs and drawings
	Labor shortages	Scope changes and claims
	Contractor or subcontractor default	Excessive owner involvement
	Theft	Operator error
	Labor productivity	Ground, structural, or equipment failure
	Work ethics	
Operation and Maintenance	Accidents	
	Inadequate maintenance	
	Natural hazards	
	Public and staff safety (general liability)	
	Malicious acts (e.g., vandalism)	
	Technology failures	
	Inability to reach desired production (performance)	
End of Life	Regulatory	
	Hazardous waste	
Cross-cutting	Inflation	Corruption and political risk
	Country economic condition	Regulatory
	Unavailability of funds, financial failure	Public objections
	Inadequate managerial skills, improper coordination between teams	Environmental pollution, excess emissions
	Lack of availability of resources	Cybersecurity
	Weather and climatic conditions	Infectious disease
		Business interruption

Source: WTW.

---

[15] Blackridge Research and Consulting. 2021. 12 Common Risks in Construction Projects. https://www.black-ridgeresearch.com/blog/common-risks-in-construction-projects; PlanRadar. 2021. 7 major risks in construction projects and how toavoid them. https://www.planradar.com/gb/builders-risk/.

Sector-Specific Risks

Transport. Much of infrastructure investment and the PRIF Pacific pipeline of projects is in the transport sector, around 56% of total project value. Transport sector projects in the Pacific countries are often close to coastlines and therefore particularly at risk from flooding due to tropical cyclones, tsunamis, and sea-level rise. Exposed projects in the Pacific pipeline of projects for 2024 onward include a port upgrade in Solomon Islands and an airport upgrade in the Cook Islands, which is situated on low-lying land close to the water. Volcanoes can interrupt air traffic.

Energy. A significant part of the PRIF portfolio includes renewable energy plant development, for example, hydropower plants in Fiji and solar projects in PNG. A key risk for these projects arises during the design stage, whereby they are required to secure a grid connection.[16] This can be exacerbated in remote areas.

Natural events such as landslides are also particularly detrimental to hydropower facilities: masses of earth and debris can contaminate water reservoirs and bury structures and thus damage facilities.[17] This is particularly true of Fiji and PNG, where landslides are common. Another risk is that while operating, expected energy production will not be met, for example, because of technological failure or climate impact as natural hazards impact performance. This risk can be mitigated and transferred to (re)insurers through innovative insurance solutions, such as parametric policies, as discussed in the next sections. Technology risk and offtake risk also apply.[18]

Water, sanitation and urban development. PRIF projects in this category include an urban water supply project in Solomon Islands, the construction of a dam in Samoa, and a sustainable urban development project in Nauru. Specific risks in this sector include that of contamination to water supplies from hazardous materials and waste, and design or operational failure leading to excess water leakage or release causing extensive flooding, also from irrigation and drainage systems. Unexpected subsurface conditions are also a key risk for water projects, where excavation is required for infrastructure such as pipelines and underground tanks. Poor subsurface conditions could change project dynamics, thus increasing difficulties, delays, and costs.[19]

Information and communication technology. Development of earthquake-triggered surrounding underwater cables is common in PRIF's ICT pipeline. These types of projects are exposed to natural hazards such as earthquake-triggered underwater landslides and volcanoes, as well as bad weather causing project delays that hinder the operation of vessels.

---

[16] Renewables First. What Are the Main Hydropower Project Risks? https://www.renewablesfirst.co.uk/renewable-energytechnologies/hydropower/hydropower-learning-centre/what-are-hydropower-project-risks/#:~:text=Detailed%20design%2Fconstruction%20stage&text=Construction%20works%20are%20normally%20conducted,the%20site%20and%20delay%20works.

[17] *Waterpower Magazine.* 2017. Hydropower's Inherent Risk Factors. 9 March. https://www.waterpowermagazine.com/features/featurehydropowers-inherent-risk-factors-5759530/.

[18] In a power purchase agreement, an "off-taker" buys power from a project developer at a negotiated rate for a specified term without taking ownership of the system. The project developer procures, builds, operates, and maintains the system. Off-take risk is the risk of not getting paid for the power output.

[19] A. Ambulkar. 2019. Top 10 Challenges in Water and Wastewater Construction Projects. Water Online. https://www.wateronline.com/doc/top-ten-challenges-in-water-and-wastewater-construction-projects-0001.

A Guide to Insurable Infrastructure in the Pacific

4

Insurance Products for Infrastructure

This section discusses insurance products suitable for insuring infrastructure risks and summarizes the available products in the 14 Pacific countries considered. It is based on interviews and literature review to identify the available (re)insurance companies that are either located in the Pacific region or provide coverage to Pacific countries. The listed insurance products address risks in the planning and design stage and the construction stage of the infrastructure project life cycle, which is when development partners generally require insurance coverage.

At a minimum, the following insurance types are typically required to meet development partners' general condition of contract for an infrastructure project, irrespective of the sector: contractors' all risk, third-party liability, workers compensation, business interruption, professional indemnity, and motor vehicle insurance. Additionally, if a project includes shipping, then a marine cargo policy would be required; likewise, if a project has workers, then adequate medical insurance would be needed. Generally, brokers will try to place contractors' all risk insurance, third-party liability, and marine cargo risks with the same insurer. They will separately place other insurance, such as motor vehicle and medical insurance, both of which can often be obtained in the local market. Table 4 reviews each of these products.

Best Practices for Contractors to Obtain Insurance

When a contractor is trying to obtain insurance for an infrastructure project, it should take the following steps:

i.   Become familiar with the development partners' insurance-related requirements for the project.

ii. Investigate the insurance legislation in the country of proposed works.

iii. Decide whether to obtain insurance directly or through an insurance broker.

It is recommended to use a broker to approach the national and international insurance markets. Brokers have more market knowledge and are more likely to know how to best access insurance to meet coverage requirements through previous insurance placements for clients, optimizing coverage at the lowest possible price. Brokers may be able to advise on the insurance legislation requirements in the country.

They will also be able to advise and coordinate the required supporting information format that insurers need. Special consideration is required for natural hazard insurance, and the option for obtaining this insurance should be explored as soon as possible, because this coverage is harder to obtain for infrastructure projects in the Pacific countries.

Table 4. Typical Insurance Policies for Contractors in the Pacific

Insurance Type	Description
Contractors' All Risks	Contractors' all-risk (CAR) insurance is intended to provide broad coverage related to the construction project but, despite its name, it does not cover all risks. Rather, it covers a list of defined hazards. CAR coverage typically includes fire, theft, accident, vandalism, water damage, construction faults, and negligence. Depending on the insurer and project, CAR coverage may or may not include natural hazards such as flood, wind, and earthquakes. CAR coverage typically does not cover normal wear and tear, willful negligence, or poor quality. Any CAR policy can be negotiated to cover additional items. While good construction practice is the first and best priority for managing risks during the construction stage, most projects cannot be executed without a CAR to cover the inevitable residual risk. In addition to a CAR policy, extra policies may be required to target more specific hazards, such as specific natural hazards, marine risks, and public liability.[a]
Third-Party Liability	Third-party liability insurance is intended to cover the contractor if a claim is made against them for personal injury, death, or damage to a third party or their property by an event during the execution of the project.
Workers' Compensation	Workers' compensation insurance covers employees of a contractor against injury and illness on the job. Notably, this policy will not cover injury outside of work (e.g., on the commute) or because of intoxication or substance abuse.
Business Interruption	Business interruption insurance covers a wide range of potential losses that arise due to delay in the construction project. It typically covers the additional cost of working and loss of profit after an event interrupts business activity. For example, delay in starting or completion of an infrastructure project can arise from property damage caused by a major storm, machinery breakdown, supply chain issues, and labor disputes.[b]
Professional Indemnity	Professional indemnity insurance protects the contractor against claims for loss or damage made because of negligent services.
Motor Vehicle	Motor vehicle insurance will generally protect the driver, vehicle, and other motorists against liability in case of an accident. Some policies may cover the mechanical failure of vehicles used in the project.
Marine Cargo	Marine cargo insurance will typically cover delays in startup, damage, loss of construction goods and materials while in transit—land, sea, or air.
Medical	Medical insurance is required for some contracting team members. This insurance should usually cover the cost of any private health care required for employees during the project timeframe.

Note: Although descriptions are provided for key insurance types, each insurer will differ in what it does and does not cover in a policy; as such, the description is provided as a guide.
[a] BuildSafe. 2022. What is Contractors All Risk Insurance and Who needs it? https://buildsafe.co.uk/what-iscontractors-all-risk-insurance-and-who-needs-it/.
[b] Marsh. 2024. Business Interruption and Supply Chain. https://www.marsh.com/uk/services/businessinterruption-supply-chain.html.

Source: WTW.

Investigate the insurance legislation of the country where you wish to conduct works

- When obtaining insurance coverage, local contractors must follow the legislation of the jurisdiction in which they propose to undertake work. For the majority of Pacific countries with a domestic insurance market, a first attempt in the local market should be made to obtain insurance before going international.

- If a contractor requires access to international insurance markets, an exemption from the government regulator must usually be sought (depending on country-specific regulations). For example, in Fiji, insurance buyers must prove that (i) no local insurer offers the policy required to cover the project; (ii) where the local insurer can offer cover, proof that they cannot obtain the levels of required insurance; and (iii) proof that the local premium, excluding stamp duty, costs more than 15% of that for offshore premium, and evidence that the local market was asked to cover the risks. Without adequate documentation (and depending on the country), this exemption process can take weeks or even months.

- It is therefore advised that contractors start seeking insurance as soon as feasible (e.g., as soon as tender details are released), and ensure all required information is prepared and submitted. While exemption from the local regulator is not always required for every type of insurance, it is required for contractors' all risk policies in jurisdictions with such regulation. Motor insurance must be sought locally. Liability insurance can usually be obtained internationally without exemption.

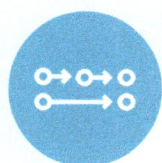

Decide whether to approach insurer directly, or through a broker

- The contractor should decide whether to approach the insurance market directly, or through a broker.

- Where insurance coverage cannot be obtained directly, it is advised to reach out to any of the multiple licensed insurance brokers operating in the region (e.g., Aon, Marsh, WTW, or IHL) to assist in obtaining adequate insurance by exploring various markets.

- It is recommended to use a broker to assist with completing the regulatory requirements for accessing the international insurance market and with presenting required risk and hazard information for insurers.

Obtain natural hazard insurance

- Disasters triggered by natural hazards insurance (e.g., tropical cyclone), aside from earthquakes and flooding (that is, unrelated to tropical cyclone), are unlikely to be covered by local insurers. Therefore, it is advised that contractors seek a contractors' all risk policy without disasters triggered by natural hazards cover and use the international market to provide catastrophe cover separately, depending on the bid requirements.

- This cover could be placed on an indemnity or parametric insurance basis, with the parametric insurance as potentially an attractive alternative to international markets. This process should be started as soon as possible, and it is advised to contract a broker/insurer to understand the documentation requirements for this coverage to avoid delays. A medium-sized contractor noted that, in recent years, it took almost a year to secure natural hazard insurance through the international market.

- If this insurance cannot be obtained, it is advised to revert to the company and/or organization that released the tender to discuss options in relation to bidding for a project without disasters triggered by natural hazards cover.

Source: WTW.

Insurance Requirements for Infrastructure

The insurance coverage matrix in Table 5 outlines insurance coverage requirements based on ADB and World Bank procurement requirements, which are largely aligned across multilateral and bilateral development partners operating in the Pacific. It lists requirements by the complexity levels common across sectors, and the table has a separate column specific to small works (less than $10 million). The insurance requirements for a consultant planning and designing civil works are different than those for a contractor only undertaking civil works. Table 5 also lists "general conditions of insurance," with corresponding types of insurance that can be used to meet the requirements, and corresponding particular conditions of contract for insurance.

For specific amounts of insurance required for the "particular conditions of contract" (e.g., minimum insurance amounts and maximum deductible amounts), development partners do not prescribe the different types or the amounts of insurance. These amounts will vary and are determined by government agencies for each project on a case-by-case basis, considering the specific circumstances of the contract. Often, government agencies will set the same insurance coverage amounts and/or deductibles for every infrastructure project for that country.

Table 5. Insurance Coverage Requirements from Development Partner Procurement Guidelines

General Conditions of Contract (insurance)	Insurance Type to Meet Requirements	Standard Contracts: Particular Conditions of Contract (insurance)	Small Contracts (<$10 million): Particular Conditions of Contract (insurance)
Insurance for Works and Contractor's Equipment	Contractors' all risk insurance	…	The minimum insurance amounts and deductibles shall be (i) for loss or damage to the works, plant, and materials: [insert amounts], (ii) for loss or damage to equipment: [insert amounts].
Insurance against Injury to Persons and Damage to Property	Property damage insurance (e.g., covers materials in transit to a site in the Pacific) Medical insurance (e.g., for expat workers)	Amount of insurance required for injury to persons and damage to property [Note: If not stated, the amount agreed with the employer]	The minimum insurance amounts and deductibles shall be (i) for loss or damage to property (except the works, plant, materials, and equipment) in connection with contract [insert amounts], (ii) for personal injury or death (a) of other people: [insert amount].
Insurance for Contractor's Personnel	Workers' compensation insurance	Maximum amount of deductibles for insurance of the employer's risks [insert maximum amount of deductibles]	The minimum insurance amounts and deductibles shall be (i) for personal injury or death, (ii) of the contractor's employees: [insert amount].
General Requirements for Insurance	Professional indemnity insurance	Amount of insurance required for liability for breach of professional duty. Period of insurance required for breach of professional duty.	…
	Public liability insurance (third-party liability)	Minimum amount of third-party insurance [insert minimum amount of third party insurance].	…
	…	Periods for submission of insurance: (i) evidence of insurance, (ii) relevant policies [insert period for submission of evidence of insurance and policy. Period may be from 14 days to 28 days].	

… = not available.
Note: Information based on Asian Development Bank (ADB) and World Bank procurement guidelines.
Sources: WTW, ADB, and the World Bank.

Development partner requirements for insurance are based largely on the International Federation of Consulting Engineers' conditions of contract (multilateral development bank harmonized conditions) and particular conditions of contract from ADB and standard bidding documents for contractors from the World Bank.[20] These and procurement guidance notes are available online for ADB[21] and the World Bank.[22]

Insurance Products Available by Country
Table 6 looks at main insurance policies available per Pacific country, the brokers operating in-country, and notes the major gaps in coverage. Appendix 1 details available policies by insurance company for each country. Sections 3 and 4 have summarized the key risks of an infrastructure project, as well as the key insurance types required to cover these risks. To assist contractors with obtaining insurance coverage for each of the identified risks in the section, Appendix 4 presents the relevant insurance policy to address the identified risk. These are illustrative mappings, and each insurer will differ on what they will cover under a given policy—these should be used as general guidance only.

---

[20]   The bid document indicates the insurance requirements to bidders. Policies and certificates for insurance will be delivered by the contractor to the project manager for the project manager's approval before the start date of the works.

[21]   ADB Conditions of Contract for Procurement of Small Works: https://www.adb.org/sites/default/files/procurementsmall-works-guide.pdf; Large Works: https://www.adb.org/sites/default/files/procurement-large-works-guide.pdf.

[22]   World Bank Condition of Contract for Procurement: https://thedocs.worldbank.org/en/doc/178331533065871195-0290022020/original/ProcurementRegulations.pdf; https://www.world-bank.org/en/projects-operations/products-and-services/brief/procurement-new-framework.

Table 6. Main Products Available in the Local Insurance Market per Country

Main Product Offerings Relevant for Infrastructure Projects	Main Brokers Operating in the Country	Major Gaps
Fiji		
Commercial vehicle third-party liability; machinery and plant; electronic equipment; commercial motor insurance; group personal accident; contract works insurance (annual cover or for single projects); liability (professional and general); marine (cargo, hull, and transit); workers' compensation	IHL is the main regional broker, other international brokers such as WTW, Marsh, and Aon can operate through IHL	Windstorm, flood, and earthquake are normally excluded from CAR policies but cover for flood and earthquake can be bought back on a case-by-case basis. Tropical cyclone insurance is not available from the local insurance markets for infrastructure projects in Fiji due to high risk, as well as the requirement of needing an engineer's certificate (which do not exist at construction phase). Projects requiring tropical cyclone cover in Fiji are advised to approach the international market, e.g., Lloyd's. Some local insurers will only offer CAR policies for noncomplex projects, such as building schools and community halls, and for Tower Insurance specifically, they will only offer CAR coverage to buildings under three stories high. Consideration of complex projects will only be given to contractors who already have policies with Tower. There is a lack of underwriting experience in machinery breakdown policies, and hence these risks are usually placed in the international market. Local insurers will generally not offer business interruption policies as delays to infrastructure projects in the Pacific are common, and this has been identified as a key risk. Additionally, worker's compensation policies are not provided locally and so will need to be sought internationally.
PNG		
Architects; and engineers; commercial motor insurance; contract works (annual cover or for single projects); design and construction; electronic equipment; group personal accident; injury or sickness; liability (CAR, professional, and general); machinery and plant; marine (hull, cargo, and transit); workers' compensation (with an extraterritorial option) industrial special risks	Kanda, Aon, Marsh, Niugini Islands, Wereck, Anitua[a]	The PNG infrastructure market is largely dominated by Chinese construction companies, and insurance is usually placed offshore after an exemption is sought, as effort must be made to obtain insurance from locally licensed insurers first. However, small residential and commercial construction projects are placed locally (less than ~$2.7 million). Underwriting expertise is limited for machinery breakdown and hence local underwriters are generally reluctant to write it. There are market limitations on available coverage for professional liability. So for professional liability insurance, individual insurer limits are $20 million; if more is needed, partnering and/or brokering is required.
Cook Islands		
Business interruption; CAR; commercial vehicle third-party liability; contract works; liabilities; marine (hull, cargo, and transit); personal accident	WTW New Zealand	Both active insurance companies (Tower and Federal) offer CAR coverage, but it is unlikely they will be able to provide full terms. Brokers often arrange a co-insurance, whereby the total limit of insurance is insured by more than one underwriter. Local insurance companies will usually take 20% of the limit, but this can range up to 80% (for example, WTW New Zealand have been known to place up to 80% of coverage with Tower). Tropical cyclone insurance is only available as an extension in the Cook Islands and is limited to those buildings with an engineering cyclone certificate that confirms the building meets the building code for cyclone. Contractors should look to place tropical cyclone cover internationally if required.
Samoa		
Business interruption; business vehicle; CAR; commercial vehicle third-party liability; contract works; liabilities; marine (hull, cargo, and transit); personal accident	Aon, Marsh, WTW	Insurance must be sought in the local insurance market.
Kiribati		
Business interruption; CAR; cargo; erection all risks; fire insurance; professional indemnity, public liability; machinery breakdown; marine (transit and vessel); workers' compensation	No licensed brokers identified through interviews	There is only one insurance company domiciled in Kiribati, called the Kiribati Insurance Corporation, and as per the Insurance Act (1981) only Kiribati Insurance Corporation can carry on insurance business in Kiribati. Although there are no/limited brokers licensed in Kiribati, this should not deter small contractors from reaching out to the usual key brokers (e.g., Aon, Marsh, WTW, and IHL), who can utilize their relationships with specialists in Kiribati and provide advice on how to achieve the required coverage.

Main Product Offerings Relevant for Infrastructure Projects	Main Brokers Operating in the Country	Major Gaps
Tonga		
Business interruption; commercial vehicle physical damage; contract works; fire insurance; liability (commercial vehicle third-party and CAR); marine (cargo and transit); personal accident; workers' compensation	WTW New Zealand	Tonga has no legislation in place to regulate its insurance industry. In the absence of a regulator, the solvency of domestic insurers, and hence their ability to pay claims and withstand shocks such as disasters triggered by natural hazards, are not assessed by any government agency. It is not possible to confirm that insurers have adequate financial security to meet any catastrophe exposures. The absence of a regulator also has implications for consumer protection, as no government agency is ensuring the appropriateness of insurance products sold in the market.
		Small contractors can bid on projects in Tonga, as they can access the international insurance market without an exemption from a regulator. Access to both the local and international markets allows for more competitive pricing than if they had to only use local insurers, which is the case for regulated environments such as Samoa.
		The low policy limits offered by local insurers for all lines of business, not just infrastructure, is demonstrated by the limited limits offered by Tower Insurance in Tonga. Therefore, it is very likely that coverage required for infrastructure projects will be obtained in the international markets.
Vanuatu		
Business interruption; commercial and/or motor fleet; commercial vehicle physical damage; fire insurance; contract works (annual cover or single project); group personal accident; liability (third-party, CAR, professional, general); machinery breakdown and electronic equipment; private vehicle; marine (cargo and hull); workers' compensation	Marsh (Fiji Office), WTW New Zealand, Aon, Chartered Pacific Insurance Brokers Ltd.	The low policy limits offered by Tower Insurance, for all lines of business, not just infrastructure, highlight the limited availability of local capacity in Vanuatu. Therefore, it is certain that coverage required for infrastructure projects will need to be obtained either partly or wholly in the international markets.
Solomon Islands		
Commercial and/or motor fleet; commercial motor insurance; commercial vehicle (physical damage and third-party liability); contract works (annual cover or single project); contractors plant and machinery; machinery breakdown and electronic equipment; marine (cargo and transit); liability (professional and general); group personal accident; private vehicle; workers' compensation;	United Risk Services Ltd., MAT Insurance Brokers Ltd., Pacific Insurance Broker Ltd., Marsh PTY Ltd.	Insurance is a major barrier for DFAT's bilateral infrastructure program due to lack of competition in the insurance market, leading to long delays in securing insurance and much higher costs. Local insurance products often are not large enough to satisfy DFAT (and other development partners) requirements, but the Government of Solomon Islands charges a 10% levy to access any international insurance.
Tuvalu, Nauru, Niue, FSM, RMI, and Palau		
No policies found	No licensed brokers	There is no local insurance company presence or local market in Nauru, Niue, Palau, FSM, and the RMI. There is no legislation in place whereby contractors operating in these countries must seek insurance from the local market first. As such, small contractors looking to obtain insurance for projects have the freedom to look for international coverage via international brokers (e.g., Aon, WTW, Marsh).
		International markets who will consider and write risk include W/R/B, HDI, and Swiss Re. Further, a large insurer in Fiji noted that a broker from Fiji will travel to these regions without a market and will place business via New India Assurance. Tuvalu pursues a self-insurance approach through a country-owned initiative, the Tuvalu Survival Fund. However, this fund is only useful for natural hazard protection and is not designed to fully indemnify losses.

CAR= Contractors' all-risk
DFAT= Australian Department of Foreign Affairs and Trade
FSM= Federated States of Micronesia

PNG=Papua New Guinea
RMI= Republic of the Marshall Islands

a Niugini Assurance (2020–2022). Directory of Independent Insurance Brokers in PNG. https://www.niuginiinsurance.com.pg/find-your-broker.

Source: WTW.

5

Value of Implementing Risk Management and Reduction Measures

Contractors bidding for works related to infrastructure projects in the Pacific and development partners designing and issuing tenders need to consider what risk management/reduction measures may be available at each stage of the project cycle. This can reduce risks under the direct control of contractors, before transferring residual risk to the insurance market, thereby increasing the chances of accessing insurance and potentially reducing premiums. Development partners and governments can also consider nature-based solutions to reduce risks.[23] For example, conserving forests, wetlands, and coral reefs can reduce the impact of disasters on communities.

It is in the interest of all parties to ensure enhanced project design incorporating risk reduction measures for more resilient and impactful investments. More sustainable infrastructure has greater socioeconomic benefits for the recipient country or borrower over the longer term and can yield cost savings by avoiding damage. Economic cost–benefit analysis is important for demonstrating the economic value of resilient infrastructure investments.

General risk management techniques can be categorized as follows: **structural** and **locational** techniques are typically "built-in" or permanent to the project and last for the duration of the project or, in the contractor's case, the duration of construction; **operational** techniques can be employed during the operation and maintenance stage. These are defined as follows:

- **Structural risk management techniques should be implemented during planning and design.** These could include designing and building sufficient strength and ductility into a structure during construction and for the life of the structure, adopting shapes that reduce loads (e.g., roof configuration against high winds), constructing flood barriers, landslide reduction, or other protective

---

23   Global Program on Nature-Based Solutions for Climate Resilience. https://naturebasedsolutions.org/.

measures to prevent or reduce peril, incorporating design elements which reflect the natural hazard risk (e.g., using specific resilient materials during construction, such as reinforced concrete to withstand earthquakes), or providing fire protection features such as onsite water supply and/or sprinklers. In essence, structural risk management involves designing and building something to withstand unwanted events.

- **Locational techniques involve avoiding unwanted events**, for example by avoiding building in mapped flood plains or areas of seismically poor soils or elevating property or structures above expected flood or tsunami heights. Poor site conditions are frequently noted as a key risk, delaying project commencement, which can be costly. Geotechnical surveys during design can manage this.

- **Operational and/or management techniques consist of improving ordinary operations to reduce the likelihood of accidents** (e.g., operator training to reduce human error); overall professional education to assure quality of planning, design, construction and operations; and emergency operations. Emergency operations are typically shorter-term

measures relative to project life, with recovery operations that can last for years after a disaster and that change the normal pattern of operations for a limited period prior, during, and after the unwanted event. Most operational techniques are short-term applications of structural measures, e.g., covering windows and roofs against wind and rain, lashing down objects against high winds, removing flammables as fires approach. They can also be locational measures, e.g., evacuation from flood, wind, fire, moving furniture to upper stories during floods, and moving boats to open water for tropical cyclones or tsunamis. A crucial factor is assessing, planning for, and applying these measures beforehand, with emergency planning and management.

Table 7 looks at key infrastructure project risks and associated risk management and risk reduction measures that can be implemented at different stages of the infrastructure project life cycle.

Risk management/reduction measures can largely be applied across the key infrastructure sectors. Table 8 provides a case study for the energy sector, listing management/reduction and structural measures that can be applied to different types of energy projects to mitigate climate impacts.

Table 7. Risk Management and Reduction Measures Across the Infrastructure Life Cycle

Life Cycle	Risk Bearer	Key Risks	Risk Management and Reduction Measures
Initiation	Project owner	Cancellation	Advocacy
Planning	Planner	Change of scope and design, feasibility, complexity	Structural risk management, client management
Design	Designer	Change in requirements, inaccurate data, design errors and omissions	Structural risk management, locational techniques, quantifying the risks, client relations, contract terms, design standards, building codes, performance-based design
Construction	Contractor	Accidents, natural hazards, delays, theft, cost overruns, inexperienced workforce	Locational techniques, construction quality management, quality assurance and quality control, construction inspection, operating manuals, client and designer relations, security
Operation and Maintenance	Project owner	Accidents, natural hazards, inadequate maintenance, lack of performance	Standard operating procedures, maintenance program
End of Life	Project owner	Regulatory, hazardous waste	Regulator relations, demolition plan and/or contractor, demolition and disposal

Sources: Pacific Regional Infrastructure Facility and authors.

Table 8. Example of Climate Risk Management/Reduction Measures in the Energy Sector

	Climate Risk Impacts	Risk Management/Reduction Measures	Structural Measure
Generation	• Inundation of coastal infrastructure, such as generation plants • Reduced efficiency of solar energy • Insufficient cooling water • Temperature of cooling water before and after use • Reduced output from hydropower generation	• Model climate impacts on existing and planned assets in collaboration with meteorological services • Revise maintenance schedules • Update hydropower operating rules	• Fortify coastal, offshore, and flood-prone infrastructure against flooding • Increase cooling system capacity for solar energy • Locate new facilities outside high-risk zones
Transmission and Distribution	• Flooding of electricity substations • Damage to transmission lines from climate extremes	• Implement program for pruning and managing trees near transmission and distribution lines • Create disaster mitigation plans • Train emergency response teams for quick repair and restoration	• Adjust design criteria for transmission lines • Increase transmission tower height • Bury distribution lines • Use stainless steel material to reduce corrosion from water damage
Consumption	• Change in energy demand patterns (e.g., increased demand for cooling and reduced demand for heating)	• Forecast load using climate information • Promote behavioral change measures to reduce peak consumption	• Improve building and industrial energy efficiency

6

Challenges of Obtaining Insurance Services

This section discusses challenges of obtaining insurance services for infrastructure projects, including risk management issues and procurement-related challenges.

Overview of Challenges of Obtaining Insurance

A significant number of contractors have noted that insurance is not always available when needed and when it is, it can be costly. Overall, contractors are increasingly challenged in obtaining affordable insurance for their projects in the Pacific. Several smaller Pacific contractors are unable to find insurance solutions. Even when insurance solutions are available, they are often prohibitively expensive and/or do not measure up to the level bidding documents require. Project owners also need to address this issue, as realistic insurance costs and availability need to be factored into overall project costs and contracts.

After the award of a bid to a contractor, the time window is limited to obtain the required insurance from the market. Time-consuming procurement practices are thus contributing to challenges of obtaining insurance at a reasonable cost, a root cause

of the problem. Changes in this engagement model and key practices are important to address this issue and allow insurers more time to evaluate projects.

Government regulations in many Pacific countries often require contractors to seek coverage in the local insurance market first to support local market development and, if not available, to look internationally. Since most of the required insurance is not available in local insurance markets, this regulation typically requires a regulator's approval, causing a bottleneck for exemption requests. These processes and government agency capacity to implement this regulation need to be reviewed and strengthened so contractors can reach international insurance markets quickly and efficiently.

Larger, international contractors are likely to have sophisticated multiproject insurance policies, which are renewed annually. Adding another project to their tender portfolio is likely to be relatively straightforward, with smaller projects having little impact on their annual premium in many cases. Smaller contractors are more likely to seek insurance on a project-by-project basis. If the project is something new or unexpectedly large or complex, existing insurance partners may be unable to support it or will require long and complex data collection to become comfortable with the change in risk profile. This naturally puts smaller local contractors at a disadvantage when tendering.

Key barriers to contractor's obtaining an insurance quote include the following:

- Insufficient information provided to the insurer combined with inconsistent or fragmented information requests from insurers.

- Lack of understanding of the risk or the physical location, including lack of a suitable risk assessment.

- Insurance transactions that are too small or on a project-by-project basis.

In these cases, an insurance quote will not be given if the data is insufficient and, if given, it will be priced higher to allow for uncertainty about the risk. In many cases, smaller contractors are unable to provide the information requested. During interviews, contractors repeatedly mentioned the limited time frames for preparing tenders and brokers confirmed that this often leads to unexpectedly high pricing or no offer of insurance.

Risk Management Issues from the Insurers' Perspective

Box 1 outlines the (re)insurer industry's view of prevalent issues in infrastructure projects in Pacific countries, which have historically deterred prospective insurers from offering adequate insurance coverage.

Box 1. Issues in the Pacific That Deter Prospective (Re)Insurers

1 **Project design does not sufficiently reflect natural hazard risk.** Design and resilience of infrastructure projects in the Pacific are significantly lower than for developed countries. This is largely due to funding, since, with less funding, projects tend to be completed with cheaper materials and with less skilled workforce. For example, roads or sea walls are often not designed with the region's natural hazard risks in mind; that is, roads or sea walls may be too low, close to the shore, and exposed to hazards such as sea surge.

2 **Project timeline does not sufficiently reflect natural hazard risk.** Development partners often set project deadlines with little consideration of the seasonality of natural hazards. This may put contractors under pressure to complete construction works during the tropical cyclone or monsoon season, for example. This makes it more difficult for insurers to price or justify cover of the infrastructure, since the project construction site and materials face greater potential for damage to equipment, buildings, etc. Insurers would prefer to focus on projects programmed with consideration and avoidance of high-risk periods to mitigate risk and increase project insurability.

3 **Limited local capacity in construction.** Local capacity and material constraints can lead to defects during construction. Materials required for an infrastructure project are often limited. For example, in the construction of a road, concrete may be in short supply, requiring sourcing of additional material from another island. If this risk is not accounted for in the timelines at the design stage, delays may result (e.g., concrete might spend more time in the mixer). It can also increase the risk of defects due to decreased quality during these delays.

4 **Accessing and navigating local legislation and regulations.** Often, insurers cannot easily determine insurance legislation and regulation in countries. This is because of difficulties in reaching government agencies responsible for regulation which leaves insurers disinclined to provide insurance in these jurisdictions. Several Pacific countries lack legislation and regulations are often opaque or lack details, which creates barriers for insurers and brokers to navigate different regulations, laws and obligations. Understanding regulations that vary among territories, including nonresidential insurance tax also takes time and resources, and thus adds to the challenge.

5 **Uncertified workforce.** Local workforce in the Pacific are not typically trained to developed country levels and lack certifications. As such, contractors appear riskier, costlier and less attractive to insurers, making it harder for them to obtain insurance from the international market.

Source: WTW.

Constraints in Insurance Requirements During Procurement

Some projects require levels of insurance coverage shaped by commercial and legal situations in developed economies. This occurs due to a lack of knowledge in governments receiving the financing for infrastructure projects (particularly for unique, once-in-a-generation projects). These insurance requirements are deemed unfeasible in some Pacific jurisdictions and can bar small contractors from bidding for projects. When contractors proceed with obtaining project-related insurance during tenders, insurers will require comprehensive project details to adequately underwrite risk. However, this detailed information is often not clear to the prospective contractor are awarded the contract. As such, it can be difficult to obtain insurance at an early stage. Further, local contractors often do not understand how to obtain the required insurance, such as who they should go to and what information and documents they need to provide. This is most often due to a lack of knowledge and information to set more suitable or targeted insurance levels and related terms and conditions.

Box 2 Example of Insurance Requirements Set Higher than Obtainable

A $20 million transport sector project in Nui-Tuvalu funded by the Asian Development Bank. Conditions of the contract required a $50,000 maximum deductible for insurance of the employer's risks, but the contractor could only get a deductible of $500,000 in the market. The original contract requirements for the deductible (set by the government) were unrealistic, given what the insurance market was prepared to offer under its available products. As a consequence, the contractor had to self-insure any loss up to the obtained deductible limit of $500,000 exposing more than if the contractor was able to negotiate a lower deductible. In this instance, the contractor was willing to offer self-insurance but not every contractor will have the financial capacity to do so.

Procurement for infrastructure projects is complex due to the number and variety of risks associated with these projects. Although risks change per type of project, in general, risk can be determined by the following factors: scale, cost, uniqueness, timeframe, and complexity. While general conditions of contracts relating to insurance are set out in development partners' bidding documents, the specific conditions of contracts include required insurance levels and deductibles set by the government implementing agency.

Procurement processes can result in a fragmented, nonuniform presentation of risk to the insurance industry, slowing down processes, disincentivizing insurers to engage, and putting pressure and responsibility on contractors. This ultimately leads to lower insurance coverage at a greater cost to the contractor.

Procurement processes can also delay engagement with contractors and the insurance sector on insurability, terms and conditions, and cost of insurance for projects. Due to a lack of pipeline visibility, insurers may also have insufficient details about the project scope and details when insurance is required, which can lead to higher premium estimates and quotes. Development partners' legal teams can amend insurance-related contract clauses, but this can prolong bidding processes and negotiation, creating pricing risks and additional costs to contractors. Reform of this engagement model would give insurers more time to evaluate projects and assess risks.

In the Pacific, governments vary in how much they pursue participation of domestic contractors, and development partners also vary their support for such approaches. While some proactively incorporate local participation in infrastructure projects, others are more averse to overt requirements. General principles in procurement policies and regulations may encourage development of local capacity, but other considerations tend to dominate at the expense of or in competition with local participation, particularly requirements for economy and efficiency. In practice, local participation thus varies. Local participation is negligible among some partners; others, such as the World Bank, actively pursue local participation given that a big share of the contracts they finance are within reach of domestic contractors. Other barriers to local involvement in infrastructure projects include a lack of local participation policy, capacity constraints such as inexperienced and poorly trained procurement personnel, and inefficient government procurement systems. Lengthy bidding creates pricing risks and adds costs to local contractors, while international contractors are more likely to be able to carry the costs from a lack of pipeline visibility and delayed project start.

Procurement teams from development partners and governments have a major part to play. This points to the importance of risk reduction measures, where risk transfer can be optimized by first reducing the underlying risk.

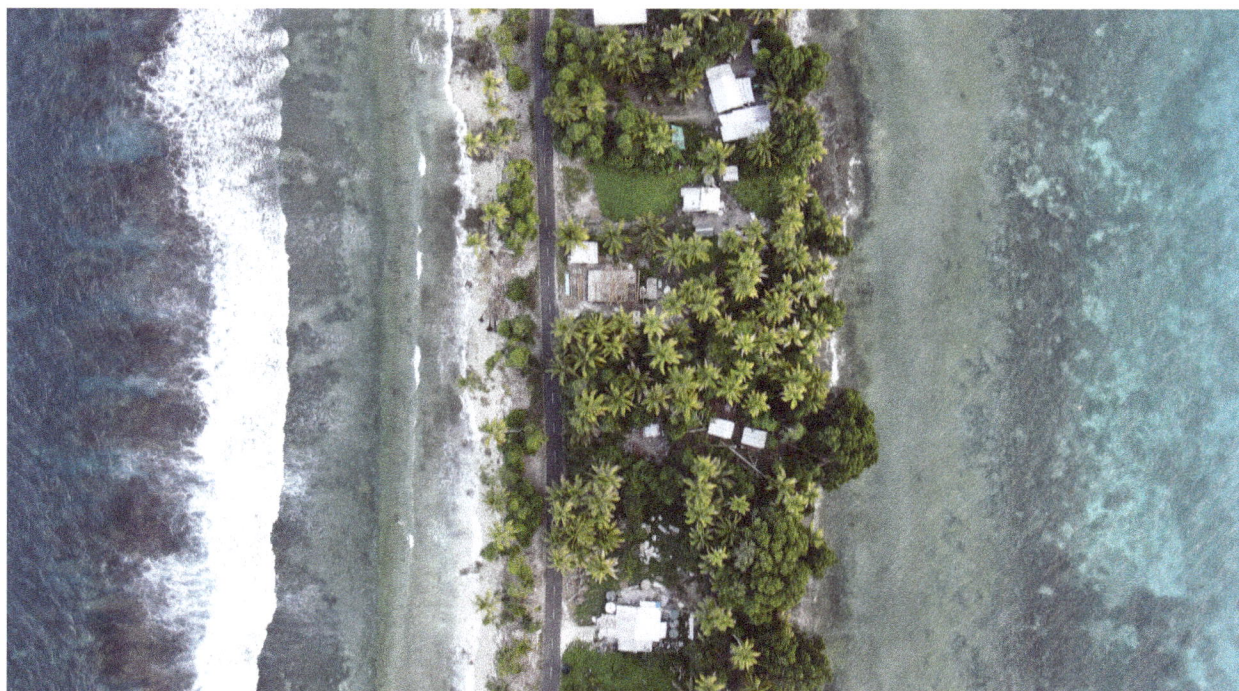

7

Recommendations for Improving Access to Insurance During Procurement

This section provides recommendations to maximize success in obtaining insurance coverage and minimize insurance premiums through enriched procurement practices, better risk management, early involvement of insurance risk advisory and de-risking services, and guidance on information to provide to the insurance industry at the optimal time.

Risk Management Good Practices

The following risk management practices can help contractors, especially local ones, become more attractive to the international insurance market and development partners to make infrastructure more resilient. Good risk management practices for project stakeholders can help address the issues discussed so far and ease access to insurance for residual risk:

- **Quantifying the risks.** Quantifying the many risks for infrastructure construction is a first step toward managing them. This is also the basis for rationally priced insurance. For example, it can include determining the probability of a specific event occurring such as a flood and its potential impact on the project. One step toward improving risk identification and quantification of construction incidents is the development of a good database of unwanted events. Problems generally arise due to poor planning in the design stage of a project. As such, a thorough risk identification, quantification, and management plan should be enforced in the early stages. (Re)insurers will tend to increase their pricing to account for the risk they expose themselves to if a contractor does not have good risk quantification methods in place, amid great uncertainty about the risks.

- **Following the building code.** In many projects, complying with the building code is seen as appropriately diligent. Contractors often prefer it since it results in the lowest possible initial capital expenditure to meet minimum requirements and specifications of building codes. Enforcement of building codes is less of a problem where they exist. However, many Pacific building codes lag in recent technical developments. They are not up to international standards, may be more applicable to buildings, e.g., residential and commercial buildings, rather than infrastructure—and may not be updated to consider climate change impacts. As a result, just complying with building codes does not lead to the lowest total project life cycle cost. The Federated States of Micronesia, Nauru, and Palau do not have national building codes. In their absence, or where codes are believed to be inadequate, efforts should be made to demonstrate to insurers that appropriately resilient materials and techniques are being incorporated in the building design equivalent to international standards, such as use of regional building codes, like those of Australia or New Zealand.

- **Performance-based design.** This refers to a standard of design where the baseline national building code requirements are exceeded for a more satisfactory design, i.e., improving upon and going beyond the minimum building code requirements. Expected losses from risks can be significantly reduced if there is additional investment to improve design, and lower overall project life cycle costs, based on assessments by design professionals. National contractors should be able to demonstrate excellent project management in the documentation submitted to insurance companies. For example, identification of material requirements at the design stage (i.e., volumes), and where these materials will be sourced. It is important for contractors to incorporate these requirements into timelines. A clear and concise management plan will be more attractive to insurers.

- **Construction quality management.** Contractors with strong governance, structures, organizational culture, health and safety practices, and quality assurance and quality control can demonstrate good risk management. For example, this includes test monitoring that provides independent inspection and material sampling to assure compliance with design documents or virtual and/or random inspections to ensure construction

materials, such as concrete, are of a good quality. Insurers, especially international ones, prefer to see evidence of quality management and risk reduction on a per project basis, rather than a manual of general risk management processes that the contractor implements across project portfolios, as each project differs. A "one-size-fits-all" approach is not recommended and contractors should avoid documents which give a generic overview of risk management or that do not differentiate risks for each project. Quality assurance, quality control, designs, and construction methods are areas that insurers consider.

Finally, self-insurance is an option in some markets where coverage is not commercially available. In this, companies knowingly bear the risk and potential loss themselves, which may include provisioning for losses by setting aside resources and taking de-risking actions. This can enable infrastructure projects to move forward in the Pacific but can result in significant costs for contractors and insolvency if significant losses occur. In this case, risk reduction and management measures are even more important to implement throughout the project life cycle to minimize the potential financial losses contractors retain. The project owner (government agencies) and development partners may need to enforce risk reduction measures. However, the number of contractors willing to bear significant financial risk through self-insurance may be limited, especially smaller contractors with limited financial reserves. With a limited pool of potential contractors willing to fully bear costs, this also reduces completion and generally raises costs. Self-insurance is generally not recommended since the contractor bears all the risk, no matter how much risk reduction, residual risk will remain.

Risk Management Advice for Development Partners

Development partners require governments to assess project-related risks in the design stage of projects or they provide assessments and guidance related to some specific project risks, e.g., climate and disaster risk. They may also require incorporation of climate resilience measures at different project stages, although risk management requirements may vary slightly across development partners. All development partners require good safety practices, such as a safety policy and standard specification for construction works on financed infrastructure projects.

Following are some specific guidance for development partners to follow related to risk management:

- **Undertake or mandate consistent risk assessment for tropical cyclone and earthquake risk** to assure underwriters that a proper and consistent risk assessment has been made, with project designs reflecting these risks. This multi-hazard risk assessment could be developed and made available through an interface for capacity building and decision-making. Development partners can also review design work by contractors to ensure it sufficiently addresses risk management issues and that seasonal and extreme weather patterns are considered in project programming and timeline. This should ease marketing of disasters triggered by natural hazards indemnity insurance and/or reduce necessary limits of parametric insurance, in both instances reducing premium costs.

- **Prepare data standards for use in catastrophe risk assessment and modeling.** Contractors, especially smaller ones, are likely unaware of how insurers and brokers assess catastrophe risk. Providing a template to present risk information in a format useful to and expected by insurers will help contractors gain insurance cover and potentially increase the number of insurers willing to take on the risk. This may reduce premiums. Stakeholders could mandate multidonor platforms to cover this activity as a centralized approach and resource.

- **Provide consistent catastrophe modeling to contractors for their use in submissions.** Doing so could ensure consistency of approach and maximize attractiveness for insurers. Design and construction standards could then be set to explicitly reflect the risk assessment. While catastrophe models may be commercially available for some hazards, benefits would be maximized if a common regional model covering key hazards (wind, flood, and earthquake) was developed, pre-discussed, and pre-agreed by leading (re)insurers. This would make each project in the pipeline more attractive, reducing risk and insurance cost. Most contractors will not have access to catastrophe modeling or ability to assess natural hazard risks. Local brokers and insurers are also unlikely to have access to catastrophe models, making placement of the disasters triggered by natural hazards risk difficult. International (re)insurers may have access to catastrophe modeling, but they are likely to take a conservative modeling stance, increasing costs. International brokers are likely to license any existing models, but not for all Pacific countries or for all hazards of interest. The creation of a consistent and regional donor-sponsored catastrophe model covering earthquakes, tropical cyclones, and floods would provide consistency and certainty. Such a model may be constructed in conjunction with interested local (re)insurers and would likely attract donor

support for development costs, for example via the Global Risk Modelling Alliance.[24] This modeling should be agreed with leading potential insurance markets in advance of an insurance placement process. Providing clarity that design and build specifications are consistent with these risk assessments would give insurers comfort and confidence. Similarly, a multidonor platform could coordinate this activity as a centralized approach and resource.

- **Support risk engineering and other risk improvement measures.** Improving on-site risk engineering assessment is important to provide a structured approach to understanding and modeling the risks the project faces. This can also include improving the capacity of professional inspection services for risk reduction. Development partners should better align the process with insurance brokers and contractors for documentation provision. For example, this would include a standard information package with standard risk assessments, following the legal and regulatory framework of each country. During the design phase of infrastructure projects and for due diligence, development partners typically use an external technical advisor or consultant, e.g., engineering consultants. It would be useful if an insurance broker were engaged during the project's technical design phase. The project management team and construction supervision team of the development partner should also be capable of ensuring risks are managed well.

- **Develop training programs in the region** to enhance local expertise in risk management, for example, to conduct professional on-site risk engineering assessments, health and safety, etc. This can help to develop local capacity through training in the design of infrastructure projects. Successful training can be rewarded with certifications recognized by insurers. Development partners generally have their own good risk management strategies in place, and this is recognized by insurers, so a certification between development partners and contractors is expected to increase attractiveness to prospective insurers. Insurers look favorably on training and

certifications as a means of reducing potential claims, as improved skills and experience has been proven effective. Training programs could help local contractors apply the relevant environmental, health, and safety safeguards and help them adhere to the requirements of development partners prior to construction, as the World Bank did in Tonga in 2015.[25]

- **Consider using SOURCE** as a multilateral digital project preparation platform promoted by the G20.[26] SOURCE facilitates early identification, evaluation, and allocation of the project's risks and impacts while enabling the monitoring of key performance indicators during implementation.[27]

Sharing Information and Timing

- **Engage brokers and the insurance industry as early as possible so they are aware of project pipelines in the Pacific.** The pipeline should include summary information, such as country and/or location, values, sector, type of insurance required, and amounts specific to each project, so the industry can start assessing appetite. For example, by sharing selected information on Pacific pipeline projects to allow the insurance industry to prepare. It is important to work with brokers to develop an organized and methodical risk transfer strategy via insurance solutions. If brokers were involved during the conceptualization of projects, they would be able to provide guidance on potential project issues and on obtaining insurance, and stating the data insurance providers need. The brokers could then advise development partners and contractors on whether alternative risk solutions were needed and what could be done to improve access to insurance. Insurers could potentially give inputs on the risk management and underwriting aspects of a project, which could help in tender design. The Pacific pipeline of projects could potentially be used for approaching the market on a risk pipeline portfolio under a regional facility discussed in Section 8.

Better risk management, the essence of this guide, will help projects, especially adaptation investments. The regional facility discussed later or a suitable insurance industry body (e.g., Pacific

[24] Global Risk Modelling Alliance. https://grma.global/.

[25] Government of Tonga. 2020. Capacity Building for Resilient Development: Application of Safeguards and 'Build Back Better' Approaches in Construction. ReliefWeb. https://reliefweb.int/report/toga/capacity-building-resilientdevelopment-application-safeguards-and-build-back-better.

[26] SOURCE. https://public.sif-source.org/source/.

[27] ADB. 2024. SOURCE – The Multilateral Platform for Sustainable Infrastructure. https://www.adb.org/publications/source-multilateral-platform-sustainable-infrastructure.

Catastrophe Risk Insurance Company [PCRIC] or Insurance Development Forum Infrastructure Task Force)[28] could be appointed for receiving and assessing this pipeline information. Where a government focuses on maximizing opportunities for its domestic construction market, which may increase risks related to the delivery of quality infrastructure due to capacity deficits and lack of access to high quality equipment and materials, it is even more critical to involve insurers early, before project designs are fixed and tenders issued. Insurers can then share their risk management and underwriting input to influence changes to the project design. Involving and supporting local contractors for smaller projects could result in cost efficiency without having to compromise quality. Contractors should involve the insurance industry (brokers and insurance providers) early in the procurement process to improve the probability that insurance is obtained.

- **Consider required information to be provided to the insurance industry by insurance policy type and timing.** Contractors should check insurers' checklists of required information in advance to increase readiness of information requests for an insurance quote, especially where local practices may differ from regional and/or global practices. Contractors should also verify policy wording in advance. Appendix 3 lists information requirements for a CAR policy.

- **Work with brokers and/or insurers to design information templates to assist the insurance placement process, pre-populated as far as possible.** This standardization will help contractors, especially smaller ones, present their risks to the market and help insurers consistently assess projects across the pipeline, likely increasing the number of interested insurers. A multidonor platform could cover this sort of activity.

- **Support capacity building of government insurance regulators and improve awareness and understanding of insurance in relation to the government approval process for accessing international insurance markets.** The aim should be for contractors to access the international insurance market quickly to reduce infrastructure project delays. The bottleneck from regulatory clearance for insurance brokers acting on behalf of the contractor to go to the international insurance market would then be quickly resolved.

---

[28] Insurance Development Forum. 2024. Infrastructure Task Force. https://www.insdevforum.org/working-groups/infrastructuretaskforce.

- **Consider signing memorandums of understanding or similar agreements with government regulators on the ability to use international insurers for a portfolio of infrastructure projects, rather than by contract.** The value of insurance or other relevant thresholds should be set nationally, above which there is no requirement to search for insurance locally.

Procurement Strategies

To address the constraints highlighted in Section 6, evaluation of development partner procurement strategies will be needed as follows:

- **Project designers should consider carving out disasters triggered by natural hazards risks, separated out from other risks where corresponding insurance types are available in the local market.** Contractors working with brokers can then determine if the insurance and reinsurance markets have appetite for taking on disasters triggered by natural hazards risks if required for the infrastructure project. Development partners should also explore the possibility of parametric insurance for insurance requirements and contractors, if traditional

indemnity insurance is not available due to concerns over building specification, standards, or claim settlements, etc. Natural hazard risks could be placed outside of a traditional CAR policy, through a stand-alone policy.

Example of a natural hazard carve out. Fiji's main natural peril exposure is to cyclones, as high winds, heavy rain, and sea surge can cause heavy damage. Windstorms are excluded from insurance unless the policyholder requests cover and pays an additional premium. Local market wordings normally contain the following exclusions: water damage unless rain enters the premises through openings caused by windstorm sea surge, high water, flood, erosion, subsidence or landslip outdoor fixtures and fittings such as solar heating equipment, satellite dishes, awnings, blinds, signs, power or telephone poles, walls, gates, and fences. Although insurers are willing to write cyclone on a full value basis, commercial policyholders normally retain the first part of every loss. A typical deductible for commercial policies would be F$1,000 ($452)[29] or 20% of the loss or damage, whichever is the greater, up to a maximum of 10% of the sum insured for any loss or damage due to gale, windstorm, hurricane, and cyclone.[30]

---

[29] Exchange rate: F$1 = $0.452 converted using Oanda FX Data Services on 27 December 2023. https://www.oanda.com/currency-converter/en/?from=FJD&to=USD&amount=1000.

[30] Fiji AXCO country report (2023).

- **Development partners can help improve in-country capacity to support contractors to better respond to procurement requirements for insurance.** They can establish procurement competency frameworks and related training programs for contractors and government (e.g., supplier engagement program) including how to bid for projects. It can include strengthening the capacity of professional associations and chambers of commerce to provide representation for local participation. For example, New Zealand Ministry of Foreign Affairs and Trade (MFAT) has been involved in providing and requesting its contractors to provide local training and capacity building for over 3 years, including requirements for health and safety, and supervision engineering for local staff.

- **For development partners with an objective of increasing local participation in projects, develop policies and use procurement mechanisms that facilitate local participation.** Incorporate local participation as early as possible into projects to allow local contractors to provide specific design advice for construction technologies and material selections that suit local markets for building as well as maintenance. MFAT already demonstrated this, for example, by having a local contractor

provide design and construction advice for the reconstruction of the Parliament House in Tonga destroyed by Tropical Cyclone Gita in 2018. These policies can also include researching the quantifiable costs and benefits of local participation to facilitate objective project decision-making. Demonstrating that higher local participation offers good value, supported by cost–benefit analysis, will strengthen the rationale for local participation. The Pacific Quality Infrastructure Principles is an important reference point guiding the way forward in terms of local participation.[31] Development partners can also consider establishing a local participation infrastructure development fund, with funds allocated for local contractors. Local contractors often lack risk mitigation measures, e.g., health and safety plans. As such, development partners and project owners need to acknowledge that health and safety planning is poor, which probably will not change in the short term, and thus they should tailor bid documents to account for this reality. Australian Department of Foreign Affairs and Trade (DFAT) and the World Bank included local contractors in establishing a routine and periodic road maintenance program. They did so through multiple methods, for example, by allowing local contractors to bid on contracts that were of a size appropriate to their current equipment and financial capacity.

---

31   Pacific Islands Forum. https://www.forumsec.org/2024/01/30/release-pacific-quality-infrastructure-principles/.

- **Development partners could split contracts or unbundle them into different work sections.** They could do this based on local contractors' skills and capacities such as separating design and build which can help local contractors bid on the phase of the project, they are qualified and can obtain insurance for. For example, DFAT has offered domestic contractors an opportunity to bid on contracts for road maintenance that were of a size appropriate to their equipment and financial capacity. By doing so, they also introduced new technology for paving roads, provided training to contractors on road maintenance, including training on bidding and tender processes for civil works, and updated key pieces of road legislation. Efforts such as DFAT's in 2010 to build capacity among the local contractors added to their experience and reduced perceived risk to insurers in future bids. Bids issued by some development partners are for design and build, while the information needed from a quantity surveyor is for design only, which is why only large players can usually participate in design and build contracts. In 2021, a project was developed in Solomon Islands for proposed works on the Malaita main road network. Only two bids were received from local civil contractors, both rejected for financial reasons. In response, a survey was undertaken by all interested national civil contractors to understand how they could change the bidding process to attract more bids. One action taken was to split three lots of proposed works into eight different contracts to target prospective bidders.

Recommendations for Government Agencies

While development partners often play a supporting role, Pacific government agencies (e.g., the ministries of finance) are responsible for implementing procurement procedures, such as issuing tenders and bidding documents, evaluating bids, managing contracts, and so forth. Government agencies also set specific levels and amounts of insurance. Development partners simply state that "reasonable" levels of insurance are needed. In most infrastructure projects, design consultants will design works, draft the bid documents for the works and construction component of the project, and set insurance requirements on behalf of the government. These are typically consultants from developed economies who directly translate their domestic policies to the Pacific island context without understanding the underlying differences and need to adapt requirements accordingly. In addition, government agencies may set the same insurance requirements as in previous efforts, even after going through a negotiation process with the previous contractor.

- **Government agencies (project owners) should review insurance requirements and amounts for projects to better understand optimal levels and adjust as needed.** Current insurance requirements (i.e., amounts of coverage) set by Pacific government agencies are causing repeated negotiations with contractors to lower these requirements for each project to feasible levels. Previous experience from contract negotiations, which reflect current insurance market conditions, should guide government agencies in setting realistic and cost-effective levels of insurance coverage. Development partners can also analyze the benefits of imposing certain insurance terms against the associated costs of the insurance, which are ultimately passed on by contractors to the project's costs, to ensure these are set at optimum levels. This can also reduce cash flow pressures on local contractors. Levels of insurance and deductibles are determined on a per project basis, and will vary by country, project size, type of infrastructure, location, etc. Levels detailed in the bidding documents should be informed by an understanding of the national, regional, or international supply market, as applicable.

For international procurement, governments generally must use the development partner standard bidding documents, which contractors use for submitting bids. For national procurement, government agencies are not required to use said bidding documents and can design and use their own more simplified bidding documents once approved by the development partner with an anti-corruption statement typically included. Some Pacific countries use their own national documents for procurement, such as Fiji and Vanuatu. However, if no template bidding document unique to Pacific countries is available for national procurement, then the government may default to the development partner standard bidding documents, which typically has many requirements for the local context. Nonetheless, the World Bank has developed a suite of simplified procurement documents, including for works.

- **Pacific countries should develop their own national bidding document templates if they have not done so already.** These should have simplified insurance requirements suitable for national procurement, which can be tailored for the broader Pacific context. Recipient governments will need guidance on how to do this with assistance from development partners.

8

Case for a Pacific Resilient Infrastructure Finance and Insurance Facility

t is difficult for local Pacific contractors to compete effectively for infrastructure projects in the region, given their limited access to affordable risk management expertise, procurement practices within development organizations, and insurance accessibility challenges. An aggregated Pacific pipeline of projects would give (re)insurers an opportunity to prepare quotes and begin to consider each project as part of a larger portfolio, rather than on a per project basis.

Role of a Potential Regional Facility

Introduction to a Regional Facility

A potential mid- to long-term solution to insurability challenges is a regional resilient infrastructure finance and insurance facility that enables pooling and international risk placement designed to cater for multiple types of infrastructure projects across the pipeline portfolio of several countries. There are various models for a risk pooling facility, but at its core it would be a donor-funded center to assist governments, development partners, and/or contractors to arrange appropriate insurance. The facility could provide support with risk assessment, modeling, standardized policy forms, and supporting documentation and information to access insurance coverage as well as mobilize private sector investors.

Regional Facility Pooling Approach

The facility could include a special purpose insurer to provide insurance to development partners, governments and potentially, via local partners, to contractors. Subject to investment in the facility— with equity, grant, or loan support provided by development partners through multilateral development partners and/or governments— and to regulatory compliance, risk may also be retained within the facility. Such risk retention by the facility could start to focus on areas where insurance is difficult or expensive to procure, such as tropical cyclone or earthquake insurance.

At the initial stage, it is likely that cover would be offered on a parametric insurance basis, requiring only a simple underwriting process. However, the facility could also act as a market for more complex indemnity (re)insurance, i.e., with other insurers following the price of leading (re)insurers after a brokered or tendered price discovery process.

Where insurance is hard to procure, the ability of the facility to offer insurance capacity will not only ensure adequate coverage is obtained but also reduce the cost of that (re)insurance placed in the regional and global (re)insurance markets, as less cover will need to be placed in a market with little appetite for the risk. Indeed, the key benefit of such a pooled approach is to reduce the cost of insurance and reduce the price volatility of the reinsurance purchased. The profit element of the premium will be retained within the facility, enabling it, over time, to either reduce premium costs and/or reduce external reinsurance purchases. Reinsurance will be purchased as necessary to protect the facility pool's capital, but the cost will be minimized, as it will be a diversified portfolio of pure Pacific natural hazard risk that is attractive to reinsurers.

Catastrophe Model Facilitation

The facility could commission the creation of a regional catastrophe model, operated by the facility, which would give regional ownership of the catastrophe model used for modeling, i.e., owned by the members of the facility. This will ensure the model is optimized to support proposed products and government needs and the consistency of modeling, encompassing all Pacific countries and all major hazards. The facility could also enable the creation of a standardized approach for risk assessment as well as tailored risk engineering surveys as appropriate to understand other risks in the project life cycle.

Procurement Process

Such a facility could work with selected brokers and international (re)insurers, with the broker curating a normal insurance placement bidding process per project with a consortium of eligible leading (re)insurers using a standardized set of policy forms and wordings. Alternatively, an insurance facility could simply be an arrangement with one or more insurers, selected by competitive tender for an agreed term to provide insurance for each project, with agreed policy wordings, pricing, and acceptance criteria.

Local Insurer Participation

A facility must allow the local insurance market to participate as required by local legislation and encourage the development of local insurance markets. It could also assist local insurers to obtain co-insurance and/or reinsurance as appropriate. It is important that the facility be seen as an enabler to local insurers, not a rival. In the short term, its role is likely to be limited to disasters triggered by natural hazards risk where there is a clear market failure.

International Insurer Participation

The international insurance industry should have early involvement in projects and provide risk advisory services. The facility can curate that process on behalf of governments, mining expertise within the international insurance markets. Importantly, the argument that risks are too small individually to interest markets can be defrayed by encouraging the insurance market to see the bigger picture of a pipeline of projects that is marketed in a standardized way using common documentation, hazard information, and, as required, modeling.

(Re)insurer Investment

The facility could also encourage (re)insurance partners to invest in the infrastructure pipeline. The insurance industry has considerable interest in developing, encouraging, and investing in infrastructure for its social purpose and to diversify investment portfolios. For example, the Insurance Development Forum, a group of insurers, brokers, and development partners, has a working group aiming to develop an Infrastructure Investment Fund.[32] Interest in developing new financial instruments is also strong, including a Pacific Resilient Infrastructure Bond, a means for insurers and others to invest. ADB's Blue Bonds show that such bonds are possible and attractive to investors.[33]

It is possible to design tender processes that reward (re)insurers who provide technical or financial support to the program without affecting price discovery, i.e., premium setting. Competitive pricing would take place (likely curated by a broker), but once a clearing price is set then the "partner" (re)insurers (i.e., more than one insurer or reinsurer) would have the first opportunity to insure a share of the risk before any final placement of insurance with local and international insurers.

---

32   Insurance Development Forum. 2024. Insurance Development Forum Announces Plans to Facilitate Investments in Resilient Infrastructure in Developing/Emerging Markets. Press release. 10 April. insdevforum.org.

33   ADB Blue Bonds September 2021. https://www.adb.org/publications/adb-blue-bonds.

Public–Private Partnership — Pooling projects into diversified risk portfolios across PICs, sectors, and financial risk management products

Risk Advisory

Early involvement in Risk Engineering Services and Disaster and Climate Risk Modeling

- Detailed checklist of all risks across the infrastructure project life cycle
- Multihazard disaster and climate risk modeling including cost–benefit analyses of adaptation investments

- Project design improvement
- Project pipeline development

De-Risking

Risk Sharing and Risk Transfer solutions for sustainable infrastructure projects

- Comprehensive "one-stop shop" insurance product offerings across infrastructure project life cycle
- Guarantees and first-loss protection structures for credit enhancement

- Lead (re)insurer with follower market
- MDB capital allocation

Quality Infrastructure

Mobilizing Private Sector Cofinancing

- Accelerated sovereign and nonsovereign mitigation and adaptation investments in line with the Paris Agreement objectives
- Development of an asset class through digitalization of project preparation

- Investment opportunities for ESG and impact investors
- Catalytic funding by donors and through MDBs

Establish a regional regulatory framework enabling the effective access to market-based financial risk management products and private sector financing via a predetermined consortium of knowledge service and financial capacity providers

ESG = environmental, social, and governance; MDB = multilateral development bank; PICs = Pacific island countries.
Source: Asian Development Bank.

Summary of Vision

Figure 3 provides a comprehensive vision for an integrated regional Pacific Resilient Infrastructure Financing and Insurance Facility. The approach under a regional portfolio of projects considers (i) risk advisory, including early involvement in risk engineering services and disaster risk modeling, (ii) de-risking through risk sharing and risk transfer solutions, and (iii) quality infrastructure investment for mobilizing private sector cofinancing.

Options for a Facility Platform

Option 1: Pacific Catastrophe Risk Insurance Company (PCRIC)

PCRIC provides parametric insurance to governments against tropical cyclones and earthquakes and is an option to host the insurance platform for the regional resilient infrastructure insurance facility. Like the other global regional risk pools, PCRIC is a not-for-profit organization set up to provide appropriate, well-priced emergency response insurance for its clients, operating in their interests while being run as a viable commercial organization.

PCRIC is owned for the benefit of the island nations of the Pacific and is a specialist provider of disaster risk finance services and solutions to the region. It delivers a program of support built on technical assistance, targeted collaborations, and innovative product options. Its mission is to help nations better prepare, structure and manage finances to foster disaster resilience and ensure rapid access to funds when they are needed most. PCRIC provides parametric tropical cyclone and earthquake emergency response risk insurance to the Cook Islands, Fiji, Niue, Tonga, and Samoa.[34]

The Caribbean Catastrophe Risk Insurance Facility (CCRIF)[35] offers disasters triggered by natural hazards insurance to public utilities on a parametric basis and other regional pools are considering similar products, which are seen as a natural extension of their current government portfolios.

PCRIC is a segregated portfolio entity, like CCRIF, which means that it can operate with more than one pot of development partner-funded capital, each supporting different products and purposes consistent with their aims and ambitions. In this case, a new cell could be created to support the provision of insurance to protect infrastructure developments, the proposed Pacific Resilient Infrastructure Finance and Insurance Facility, through investments by development partner grants or loans. Such a cell could be created at a very low cost and share the organization and infrastructure of PCRIC, making it an option. PCRIC recently updated its regulations to offer insurance for nonsovereign entities, making it possible to engage with contractors and construction business associations.

Like the other regional risk pools, PCRIC has a small executive team, outsourcing functionalities such as insurance company management and technical product development. As such, it is better suited, in the short term, to support the provision of a parametric insurance product which could use the same underlying catastrophe modeling as its core emergency response program. The policy form will be different to an emergency response program but, being a parametric program, the underwriting process will be similar.

The catastrophe model previously used by PCRIC is, however, of an elder generation, difficult to maintain, and does not fully reflect the current risk landscape. The hazard model did not account for recent loss events and current views of climate change, and the exposure model did not take into account population and wealth changes over the last 10+ years. PCRIC is in the process of implementing new models for tropical cyclone, excess rain, earthquake and tsunami and may be willing to extend its new modeling to cover infrastructure risks. While the modeling output

for emergency response insurance and infrastructure insurance may be different, the representation of hazard, a core element of the model, is common. It is likely that the infrastructure cell would be run separately initially, determining and purchasing its own reinsurance. However, it would be possible to place reinsurance in conjunction with PCRIC's own reinsurance placement, obtaining economies of scale and gaining maximum benefit from diversification. One prominent development partner has allocated significant funding to existing regional risk pools, including PCRIC, to provide appropriate support to enable them to grow and thrive.[36] The cost of reinsurance and catastrophe bonds spiked in 2022 following a series of large catastrophes, making it difficult for regional risk pools to hold pricing. One consideration is how to reduce the cost of reinsurance to the existing regional risk pools and to provide protection against reinsurance price cycles and post-loss price increases.

This outlined option of a pooling mechanism could be developed to share risk using PCRIC, local insurers, and international reinsurance and capital (catastrophe bond) markets. Indemnity insurance is currently beyond the scope of PCRIC's offerings but could be explored over the longer term, perhaps PCRIC acting as a consolidator, packing business for PRIF and its members, and, if required, fronting for international insurers.[37]

PCRIC is well established and has regional reach. Its presence as part of the facility could make support from Pacific governments, especially potential regulatory changes and/or exemptions, easier to obtain if necessary. However, political will and commitment from Pacific governments would be required. PCRIC is also donor-funded, thus any donor concerns about funding private insurer profit would need to be addressed.

Option 2: Government-Led Country Portfolio Insurance Approach

In development partner bidding documents, there is an option for governments to purchase insurance themselves for funded infrastructure projects. Governments can consider insuring infrastructure projects on a country-level portfolio basis, rather than contractors trying to insure individual projects. Governments will then take on some of the risk themselves and approach the insurance market with

---

34 Pacific Catastrophe Risk Insurance Company. https://pcric.org/.

35 Caribbean Catastrophe Risk Insurance Facility (CCRIF). https://caricom.org/institutions/caribbean-catastrophe-risk-insurance-facility-ccrif.

36 Global Shield. Available from: https://www.globalshield.org/news/events/launch-of-the-global-shield-programme-forresilient-risk-pools/.

37 See Investopedia. https://www.investopedia.com/terms/f/fronting-policy.asp.

a portfolio of several projects, enabling a spread of the risk and lower costs. This has been an option in bid documents for a long time; however, Pacific governments have not previously utilized this option to insure projects. This likely has been considered too difficult with government agencies not familiar with the process to obtain the required insurance, so the onus is currently put on contractors. Hence, this option would require some training and capacity building to implement. Ministries of finance would be a good focal point for this option, given that the ministries are usually responsible for handling other types of government insurance, e.g., protection of government public assets from disasters triggered by natural hazards.

The financing of the insurance would also be an issue. Would elements of the cost be covered by government and/or costs passed down to contractors, and, if the latter on what basis would the cost split be made?

This option can bring efficiency gains and cost savings by approaching the insurance market with a country portfolio of projects instead of the current per project approach. A centrally created facility could explicitly help governments in this process, should they prefer this approach. This could be combined with the pooling approach the two methods are not mutually exclusive.

Buying insurance for one country is likely to be more expensive than pooling risk across the Pacific and buying (re)insurance collectively, benefiting from diversification of risk and so lower insurance pricing.

Option 3: Development Partner-Led Portfolio Insurance Approach

Development partners could consider buying out natural hazard risk centrally, thus reducing costs by presenting a portfolio of risks to the market, giving scale and diversification benefits, and also increasing attractiveness. Coupled with consistent and credible risk modeling, premiums both on a portfolio and marginal project basis will be reduced assuming the risks are appropriately brokered in the widest possible market. Local procurement rules will need to be observed, ideally through early discussion with regulators before the individual project is marketed and added to the policy. Contractors could be required to accept this insurance and/or have the option to replace it with their own insurance policy giving at least equal levels of cover. For instance, rules will need to be pre-agreed if cover needs to be extended due to construction delays.

The purchase of natural hazard risk centrally would ideally use consistent catastrophe risk modeling and a common policy form. Insurance could be purchased on a parametric or indemnity basis, bundling projects as appropriate. Potential insurers would be made aware of the pipeline of projects that could generate broader market interest and lower per project costs. The cost of this insurance could be funded or covered in bids. If central purchase is deemed impossible or undesirable, then, as a minimum, common modeling, policy forms, information packs, and placement guidance could be developed to assist contractors and their brokers

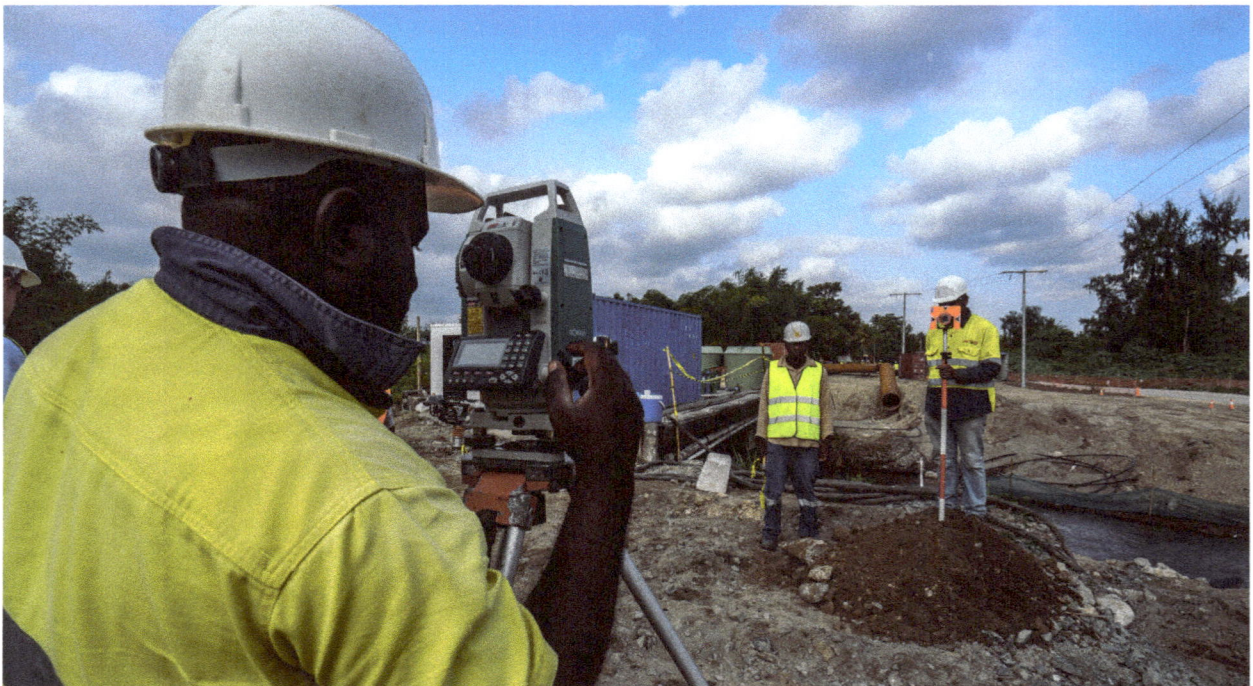

to arrange insurance to cover the disasters triggered by natural hazards risk. If the policies are parametric, then local insurer appetite is likely to be low, given the general lack of experience with parametric insurance products, expediting exceptions to allow international placement.

For development partners to bear some of the project risks on a project portfolio basis, this approach would need a financing mechanism or means to pay insurance premium costs, since development partners are constrained by certain financing instruments, e.g., project financing, policy-based financing, etc. Through a development partner-led portfolio insurance approach, development partners can potentially finance the insurance premium costs directly, rather than the current approach of being passed on indirectly by contractors as project costs. However, the insurance costs need to be directly

attached to the project as eligible expenditures. As such, insurance premiums could be added to the list of eligible project expenditures.

Summary of Options

There is no right or wrong approach, but the benefits of cooperation, commonality, sharing model development, coordinating risk placement, and getting the benefits of diversification via risk pooling are compelling. Each option comes with its challenges. Probably the simplest to achieve would be to encourage and support governments and/or development partners to place insurance collectively, perhaps supported by a regional facility. But maximum benefits would be obtained by a true regional Pacific Resilient Infrastructure Financing and Insurance Facility approach, starting first with the most difficult form of insurance to place, disasters triggered by natural hazards insurance.

Table 9. Benefits and Disadvantages of a Regional Facility Approach

BENEFITS

Attractive to local, regional, and international contractors, insurers, and other relevant market participants, since this would enable a single point of contact for market participants and a single source of information of the project pipeline. A single facility pool can also encourage international best practice in risk reduction.

Local and regional insurance companies can be encouraged to grow and expand. At the same time, access for international insurers to insurance projects can be widened on commercial terms. Packaging infrastructure project insurable risks and offering these on a portfolio basis to the insurance industry can encourage more competition and bring more markets in, lowering premium prices.

Ease insurance supply in the region by attracting more competition and bringing in more insurers by pooling infrastructure risks through one facility. This can achieve economies of scale, lowering costs, and increasing the pool of premiums available. Potential vehicles include a protected cell company or a segregated cell company (e.g., under the host platform), a captive or mutual insurance company.

Could help avoid issues of selection bias, whereby only the better quality or lower risk projects, and larger projects can get insurance.

Could improve access to insurance by writing policies, possibly subsidized, that enable a local contractor to buy out that deductible at affordable terms through another insurance policy. High deductibles lower the cost of insurance but can be a financial risk that is beyond smaller, local insurers, excluding them from participation in projects.

More standardized, and greater consistency of information required for providing insurance, which is more efficient and easier for both contractors and insurers.

Potential to minimize costs by cooperating with PCRIC, an existing development partner-supported, not-for-profit, regional parametric insurance provider.

Could provide a risk advisory function, which will allow the key value proposition of the insurance industry to be leveraged at an early stage, i.e., understanding of the risk along the project life cycle and considering climate change scenarios, strengthening the design of the projects and the project pipeline itself. Capacity building can be provided for local contractors and insurers.

DISADVANTAGES

Time and resources (including development partner funding) would be required to develop technical and administrative capacity of the host agency for the facility, including product development, research and development, advocacy, and gaining political support in the region, capitalization of a new cell, etc.

Company (or cell within PCRIC) will need capitalization and potentially, premium support, if the facility offers insurance to Pacific countries.

Risk that a poorly designed facility competes with or shuts out existing successful providers in the regional insurance sector. Careful engagement with local and regional insurers are required to ensure that this is not a perception, still less a reality. The facility needs to encourage local market development.

Appetite for such cooperation and practical issues around implementation and operation remain to be determined.

9
Conclusion

The insurance industry and its value proposition can help countries build the needed infrastructure that can boost economic resilience, overcome poverty, and meet the challenges of climate change. Insurance can defray the many daunting risks inherent in infrastructure projects exposed to disasters triggered by natural hazards and other risks. This is perhaps nowhere truer than in the Pacific, where a confluence of disaster risks from earthquakes and volcanoes to weather-related risks compounded by climate change calls for a much wider use of insurance products.

Disjointed and ill-informed efforts to obtain insurance, made worse by high project costs and risks in the Pacific, have led to a pronounced market failure, impeding much required infrastructure development. Addressing this market failure demands that development partner, governments, contractors, and insurers cooperate to find a new way forward.

The guide has aimed to improve knowledge in the region of insurance and of its barriers and benefits. It has presented a conceptual framework for obtaining insurance for infrastructure projects in accordance with industry best practices.

Its recommendations can enable the insurance industry to enter infrastructure projects early to better identify and address risks, governments and other authorities to design better policy and regulation, and to help local contractors navigate a complex process to obtain insurance and bid successfully on infrastructure projects.

This calls for a fundamental shift in practices, with early and proactive engagement of the insurance industry in the project life cycle. It demands that stakeholders embrace options like a pooled risk approach that can practically and effectively aggregate project portfolios in the Pacific.

The concept of solidarity and risk diversification across the region's various countries including different sectors and all type of risks—without anti-selection of difficult risks or cherry-picking good risks only— will lead the way out of risk concentration and can bridge the insurability gap in the Pacific and help infrastructure projects from inception through planning and design, better positioning them for completion and maintenance. De-risking infrastructure by enhancing the design and transferring risk across the life cycle of projects will enable mobilization of various sources of urgently needed financing, including investment from the insurance industry's asset management side, and governments can more easily align with the Sustainable Development Goals and meet their Paris Agreement commitments.

Importantly, the Pacific's unique challenges call for a tailored solution. In this, a resilient, regional ifacility offers a viable mechanism to improve insurability and foster collaboration across borders. Such a facility could streamline risk assessment, standardize insurance coverage, and mobilize private sector financing, helping to achieve the economies of scale that infrastructure often demands.

Through better risk management, innovative financing mechanisms and collaborative partnerships, all of the many stakeholders that surround infrastructure projects can help create more resilient economies and achieve prosperity within the Pacific.

Appendixes

Appendix 1
Active Insurance Companies by Country and Their Relevant Product Offerings

The table in this appendix details insurance products by country. This is not intended to be an exhaustive list; rather it is a list of all policies that were found from online sources and through engagement with different stakeholders.

ALPHA INSURANCE & SURETY COMPANY INC.

PNG

Air meet liability	Group injury and sickness	Protection and Indemnity
Aircraft	Industrial special risks	Public and Product
Airport contractors	Kidnap and ransom	Refueling equipment
Bankers blanket bond	Marine Cargo (Charterer's, Stevedore's, Ship Repairer's, Wharfinger's, Shipping Containers Ship Agent's, Carrier's)	Riots
Burglary and money		Salary continuance and make-up pay
Contract works (all risks)		Strikes and civil commotion
Corporate travel insurance	Marine hull	Tamper
Crime manager liability	Mobile plant and equipment	Terrorism and looting
Excess	Other specialist aviation products	Transport and liability
Extension	Premises	Worker's compensation (common law and statutory cover)
Extraterritorial	Professional indemnity (accountants, architects and engineers, design and construction, IT combinations, fund manager, recruitment consultant)	
Flood		Worker's emergency transportation and hospitalization abroad
General property		
Ground handling equipment and liability		

> Continued on next page

CAPITAL INSURANCE GROUP

Fiji

Burglary
Contractors' All Risk
Contractors plant and machinery
Commercial/motor fleet/private
vehicle
Commercial property
General property
Fidelity guarantee
Machinery breakdown
Marine and cargo transit
Money
Public and product liability
Workers compensation

Solomon Islands

Burglary
Contractors' All Risk
Contractors plant and machinery
Commercial/motor fleet/private
vehicle
Commercial property
General property
Fidelity guarantee
Machinery breakdown
Marine cargo and transit
Money
Public and product liability
Small business
Workers compensation

PNG

Burglary
Contractors' All Risk
Contractors plant and machinery
Commercial/motor fleet/private
vehicle
Commercial property
General property
Fidelity guarantee
Machinery breakdown
Marine cargo and transit
Money
Public and product liability
Small business
Workers compensation

Tonga

Burglary
Contractors' All Risk
Commercial/motor fleet/private vehicle
Commercial property and money
General property
Marine cargo and transit
Public and product liability
Small business
Workers compensation

Vanuatu

Burglary
Contractors' All Risk
Commercial/motor fleet/private vehicle
Commercial property and money
General property
Machinery breakdown and electronic
equipment
Marine cargo and transit
Public and product liability
Small business
Workers compensation

FEDERAL PACIFIC INSURANCE

Cook Islands

Business interruption
Contractors' All Risk
Liabilities
Material damage (commercial cover or
buildings, contents, stock and equipment)
Marine hull
Marine cargo and transit
Personal accident

Samoa

Business interruption
Contractors' All Risk
Liabilities
Material damage (commercial cover for
buildings, contents, stock and equipment)
Marine hull
Marine cargo and transit
Personal accident

Tonga

Business interruption
Contractors' All Risk
Liabilities
Material damage (commercial cover for
buildings, contents, stock and equipment)
Marine hull
Marine cargo and transit
Personal accident

Vanuatu

Business interruption
Contractors' All Risk
Liabilities
Material damage (commercial cover for
buildings, contents, stock and equipment)

Marine hull
Marine cargo and transit
Personal accident

FIJICARE INSURANCE

Fiji

Public liability

PACIFIC MMI INSURANCE LIMITED

PNG

Commercial/Corporate Insurance

KIRIBATI INSURANCE CORPORATION

Kiribati

Business interruption
Cargo insurance
Contractors' All Risk
Erections all risks
Fire
Machinery breakdown

Marine transit
Marine vessel
Workmen compensation
Professional indemnity
Public liability

> Continued on next page

QBE PACIFIC ISLANDS

Fiji	Solomon Islands	PNG
All risks for movable goods and equipment Burglary Business interruption Electronic equipment Commercial motor Commercial property Contract works insurance for annual cover or for single projects General liability Glass Group personal accident Machinery and plant	All risks for movable goods and equipment Burglary Business interruption Electronic equipment Commercial motor Commercial property Contract works insurance for annual cover or for single projects General liability Glass Group personal accident Machinery and plant	All risks for movable goods and equipment Burglary Business interruption Electronic equipment Commercial motor Commercial property Contract works insurance for annual cover or for single projects General liability Glass Group personal accident Machinery and plant

Vanuatu		
All risks for movable goods and equipment Burglary Business interruption Electronic equipment Commercial motor Contract works insurance for annual cover or for single projects	Commercial property General liability Glass Group personal accident Machinery and plant Machinery breakdown and electronic equipment	Marine local transit Money Property Professional liability Public and product liability

SAMOA SURETY INSURANCE

Samoa

Business Vehicle Insurance
Commercial (disasters triggered by natural hazards)

SUN INSURANCE

Fiji

Burglary Commercial fire Contractors' All Risk	General Insurance (e.g., motor, home owners and commercial) Marine hull and cargo Public liability

TOWER INSURANCE

Cook Islands	Fiji	Samoa
Business liability Business loss of income or profits Business money Business property Business property breakdown Burglary Commercial vehicle physical damage Commercial vehicle third-party liability Contract works Employee fraud	Burglary Business property Business liability Business property breakdown Commercial vehicle physical damage Commercial vehicle third-party liability Contract works	Business liability Business loss of income or profits Business money Business property Business property breakdown Burglary Commercial vehicle physical damage Commercial vehicle third-party liability Contract works

Solomon Islands	Tonga	Vanuatu
Business liability Business loss of income or profits Business money Business property Business property breakdown Burglary Commercial vehicle physical damage Commercial vehicle third-party liability Contract works Employee fraud	Business liability Business loss of income or profits Business money Business property Business property breakdown Burglary Commercial vehicle physical damage Commercial vehicle third-party liability Contract works Employee fraud Fire	Business liability Business loss of income or profits Business money Business property Business property breakdown Burglary Commercial vehicle physical damage Commercial vehicle third-party liability Contract works Employee fraud Fire

PNG=Papua New Guinea

Appendix 2
Matching Identified Project Life Cycle Risks with Insurance Products

Contractors' all-risk (CAR) insurance may apply to several risks identified in this table, depending on the terms and conditions of the specific CAR policy, and available additions. Also, a CAR policy should be purchased to address most infrastructure project risks, but specific policies can additionally be bought to target more specific risks that may be excluded from a CAR policy (e.g., disasters triggered by natural hazards, political risk, and business interruption cover).

Many of the identified risks in the table are "business risks" and may not normally be insurable or have directly associated insurance products until there is negligence, in which case professional indemnity could be an appropriate insurance type. There could also be customized insurance solutions for risks without directly associated products, which should be discussed with prospective insurers where applicable. Business interruption insurance is typically against hazards covering property damage. (Sub)contractor default risk may be separately addressed by construction surety bond products e.g., bid bonds, supply bonds, performance bonds, payment bonds. These bonds also enhance the creditworthiness of the contractor.

Life Cycle	Risks	Potential Insurance Product
Initiation	Cancellation of project	Customized insurance solutions
Planning	Scope and design changes	Professional Indemnity
	Scheduling errors, contractor delays	Business Interruption
	Cost overrun	Business Interruption
	Loss of paperwork (e.g., contract by theft, carelessness or misplacement)	Professional Indemnity Theft, Burglary Policy
	Technical feasibility	Professional Indemnity
	Economic viability	Professional Indemnity
	Inadequate scope of work	Professional Indemnity
	Project complexity	General/Third-Party Liability
	Material provision	Cargo Business Interruption
	Inadequate selection of contract types (e.g., lump sum, unit price, cost plus, etc.)	Professional Indemnity
Design	Design errors and omissions	Professional Indemnity
	Overruns anticipated timeframe	Business Interruption
	Stakeholders request late changes	Delay in Start-up
	Non-abidance of the design contract	Professional Indemnity
	Loss of paperwork	Theft, Burglary Policy Professional Indemnity
	Inaccurate data	Professional Indemnity
	Nonpayment by owner	Surety Bond; Trade Credit
Construction	Property cost overruns	Contractors' all-risk (CAR)
	Technology changes	CAR
	Inflation	Customized insurance solutions
	Inadequate managerial skills, improper coordination between teams	CAR Professional Indemnity
	Poor safety procedures/accidents	CAR Professional Indemnity Medical Insurance Policy

> Continued on next page

Life Cycle	Risks	Potential Insurance Product
	Injury to public and/or workers	CAR Workmen's Compensation Public Liability
	Natural hazards (e.g., tropical cyclone, earthquakes, flooding)	Disasters triggered by natural hazards policy Business Interruption
	Inexperienced workforce	Professional Indemnity
	Labor shortages	Customized insurance solutions
	Subcontractor default	CAR
	Theft	CAR Theft Burglary Policy
	Labor productivity	Customized insurance solutions
	Work ethics	Customized insurance solutions
	Wage scales	Customized insurance solutions
	Delays (e.g., in possession of site, design/drawings, materials, completion)	CAR Professional Indemnity
	Problem with site conditions (e.g., soil, utilities)	CAR Third-Party Liability Professional Liability
	Noise, fumes, and dust	CAR Third-Party Liability Environmental Liability
	Hazardous waste	CAR Third-Party Liability Environmental Liability
	Defective materials	Professional Indemnity
	Delays in designs/drawings	Delay in Start-up
	Errors in design and drawings	Professional Indemnity
	Scope changes and claims	Professional Indemnity
	Operator error	Workers' Compensation Injury/Sickness
	Ground, structural, or equipment failure	Professional Indemnity Machinery and Plant, Electronic Equipment
Operation and Maintenance	Accidents	Workers' Compensation Injury/Sickness Third-Party Liability
	Inadequate maintenance	Professional Indemnity
	Natural hazards (e.g., tropical cyclone, earthquakes, flooding)	Industrial Special Risks Disasters triggered by natural hazards policy
	Public/staff safety	General/Third-Party Liability
	Malicious acts	Vandalism Terrorism Political Risk Policies Active Assailant Loss of Attraction Strikes, Riots and Civil Commotion
	Lack of performance	Customized insurance solutions
	Technology failures	Customized insurance solutions
	Inability to reach desired level of production	Customized insurance solutions

> Continued on next page

Appendixes

Life Cycle	Risks	Potential Insurance Product
End of Life	Regulatory	Customized insurance solutions
	Hazardous waste	Third-Party Liability Environmental Liability
Cross-Cutting	Inflation	Customized insurance solutions
	Country economic condition and rules and regulations	Customized insurance solutions
	Unavailability of funds, financial failure	Customized insurance solutions
	Inadequate managerial skills, improper coordination between teams	CAR Professional Indemnity
	Lack of availability of resources	Customized insurance solutions
	Weather and climatic conditions (e.g., tropical cyclone, earthquakes, flooding)	CAR Disasters triggered by natural hazards policy Business Interruption
	Corruption and political risk	Vandalism Terrorism Political Risk Policy Active Assailant Loss of Attraction SRCC
	Regulatory	Customized insurance solutions
	Public objections	Professional Indemnity
	Environmental pollution	Third-Party Liability Environmental Liability

Source: WTW.

Appendix 3
Information to Be Provided to an Insurer at an Early Stage for Contractors' All Risk Policy

Information Requirements	Details
Project name and location of site	
Description of contract work	• dimensions (length, height, depth, spans, number of floors) • foundation (method, level of deepest excavation) • construction methods • construction material • contract value
Is the contractor experienced in this type of work or construction method?	
Work to be carried out by subcontractors	
Period of insurance: estimated construction period (months)	commencing from and to
Subsequent maintenance period	commencing from and to
Give full details regarding	• fire • explosion hazard • blasting work • earthquake • other risks • subsoil conditions (rock, clay, gravel, sand, filled ground) • other subsoil conditions • groundwater level
Name and distance nearest river, lake, or sea	
Levels of such river, lake, or sea:	• low water • mean water • highest level ever recorded
Level of deepest excavations	
Meteorological conditions	• rainy season, from, to • max rainfall (mm) per hour, per day, per month • storm hazard: minor, medium, high
Are there any existing buildings or surrounding property possibly affected by the contract works (excavating, underpinning, piling, vibrating, ground water lowering, etc.)?	
Are extra charges for overtime night work, work on public holidays to be included?	If so, limit of indemnity?
Is third-party liability to be included? Has the contractor concluded a separate policy for third-party liability?	If so, limit of indemnity?
Please state hereunder the amounts you wish to insure, and the limits of indemnity required	
Section 1 – Material damage	Items to be insured, state sum insured for each: • contract works (permanent and temporary work including all materials to be incorporated herein) • contract price • materials or items supplied by the principal • construction plant and equipment (attach list of items) • construction machinery (attach list showing replacement values of new items) • clearance of debris (insured only up to amount indicated) • professional fees • total sum insured Special risks to be insured, state limits of indemnity: • tropical cyclone, earthquake, volcanism, tsunami
Section 2 – Third-party liability	Items to be insured, state limits of indemnity for each: • bodily injury, any one person, total • property damage, total limit to be applied

mm = millimeter.
Source: WTW.

Appendix 4
Contractors Operating in the Pacific by Project Value

Contractor Category	Approximate Project Value Range	Examples
Local contractors	<$20 million	Ca'Bella Pacific Construction (Samoa and Tonga): Work on wharfs, bridges, and water tanks, but mainly focus on less complex assets such as: government buildings, warehouses, hotels, and health care facilities.[a] Fletcher Construction (Vanuatu): Work on projects such as wreck removals and repairs to wharfs.[b] Higgins (Fiji): Provide civil construction services across New Zealand and the Pacific. This includes road, rail, renewable energy, and airport construction projects.[c] Lorma Construction (PNG): Specialize in roads, highways, bridges, airports, commercial and residential buildings, aggregate production, material testing, and plant hire.[b]
Medium-sized international contractors	$20 million–$50 million[e]	Downer (Australia and New Zealand): Work in transport, utilities, facilities, industrial, and energy infrastructural sectors.[f] Hall Contractors (Australia): Work on dredging, flood mitigation, harbors, and marina projects. They can subcontract, but usually tend not to. Currently active in Tuvalu and have prospective projects in Kiribati and the Republic of the Marshall Islands. Reeves International (Australia): Work on wharf, desalination, water treatment, and water tank projects. They subcontract to local contractors regularly.
Large international contractors	$50 million	China Railway Construction Corporation Ltd (Global): They cover project contracting, planning and design, construction, supervision, operation and maintenance, investing and finance for railways, highways, bridges, tunnels, and urban rail transit. They operate in PNG, Cook Islands, Tonga, Vanuatu, and Fiji.[g] McConnel Dowell (New Zealand, Pacific Islands and Australia): Work on projects in: transport, ports, water and wastewater, energy, resources, and buildings.[h] They are active in Tonga on a wharf reconstruction project.

PNG = Papua New Guinea.

Note: Categorization of project size is approximate and based on discussions with contractors.

a   Ca'Bella Pacific Construction. 2024. http://www.cabellasamoa.com/portfolio/.
b   Lorma. 2023. https://lorma.com.pg/.
c   Vanuatu Project Management Unit. 2024. Fletcher Wins Lenakel, Litzlitz Contract. https://vpmu.gov.vu/index.php/news/196-fletcher-wins-lenakel-litzlitz-contract/.
d   Higgins. 2023. https://www.higgins.co.nz/what-we-do/projects/.
e   Estimate taken from interviews with medium-sized international contracting firms.
f   Downer Group. 2024. https://www.downergroup.com/.
g   China Railway Construction Corporation Limited. 2023. https://english.crcc.cn/col/col21582/index.html.
h   McConnel Dowell. https://www.mcconnelldowell.com/.
Source: WTW.

Appendix 5
People Interviewed, October–December 2023

Organization	People Interviewed
Asian Development Bank	• Sarah Colacci, senior procurement specialist • Thomas Kessler, principal finance specialist – disaster insurance
Department of Foreign Affairs and Trade (Australia)	• Emma Tiaree, local content lead • Peter Kelly, infrastructure advisor • Samuel Bunt, private sector team
Australian Infrastructure Financing Facility for the Pacific	• Lasale Cocker, investment implementation director • Tim Simpson, environment and social safeguards and project implementation
Government of Kiribati	• Ereta Turaki, senior procurement officer
Hall Contracting Pty Ltd	• William Blank, associate director development • Daniel Grey, general manager marine infrastructure
Infratec	• Henry Sommerville, senior project manager
Insurance Development Forum	• Joe Wee, chief underwriting officer and head of engineering lines, Zurich Insurance
Insurance Holdings (Pacific) Limited Fiji	• Ilyaz Koya, head of broking • Jason Nili, general manager • Sarah Chand, senior account manager
Japan International Cooperation Agency	• Asano Yoko, consultant, international development • Shigeru Sugiyama, grant project procurement • Akira Fujiwara, loan project procurement
Ministry of Foreign Affairs and Trade (New Zealand)	• Katrina Murison, lead advisor infrastructure • Jonathan Suggate, lead advisor energy • Zoe Genet, legal advisor • Michael Ball, project delivery manager • Ryan Ingleton, senior commercial advisor
Pacific Catastrophe Risk Insurance Company	• Lotu Palu, chief executive officer • Pankraj Singh, finance and planning manager
Pacific Regional Infrastructure Facility coordination office	• Jane Romero, technical assistance officer
Reeves International, Inc.	• Simon Gorman, managing director • David Fair, operations and compliance manager
Sun Insurance Fiji	• Avikash Ram, manager underwriting • Tarlochan Singh, principal officer
Swiss Re Group	• Rob McNab, senior engineering underwriter • Bo Jiang, head of public sector solutions • Christian Wertli, head of infrastructure solutions • Gerry Lemcke, head of product management • Ester Kim, senior product manager
Tower Insurance Fiji	• Veilawa Rereiwasaliwa, director
The World Bank	• Michael Osborne, procurement hub leader • Cris Nunes, senior procurement specialist
WTW Australia	• Iain Drennan, regional construction leader Australasia • Mark Thompson, construction broking leader Australasia
WTW New Zealand	• Cedric Suifua, client director

Source: WTW.

Glossary

The following key terms have been defined in the context of infrastructure insurance.

Broker	Person or company who acts as the intermediary between an insurer and a client, to advise and arrange insurance.
Co-insurance	Instances where more than one insurer accepts a percentage of the total policy limit, for a defined risk. For example, a policy limit of $100 million might be shared by three insurers as follows: Insurer A (50%), Insurer B (25%), and Insurer C (25%).
Construction insurance lead	Principal (re)insurance company(ies) in a region that offers construction insurance.
Contract works insurance	Insurance that typically protects the policyholder against accidental loss, damage, or destruction to the work in progress on a building site. It can cover the cost of repairing building work on a construction site and is usually provided on an "all risks" basis, referred to as a "contractors' all risk insurance" policy.[1]
Contractor	Person or entity who supplies materials or workers to perform a service or job.[2] In this guide, a contractor is referred to as the person or entity employed to undertake the construction of works.
Deductible/excess	Monetary amount that the policyholder must pay toward an insurance claim.
Development partners	Refers to any organization working in partnership with national and/or local government bodies. In this guide, "development partners" may also include donors.
Established markets	Markets where insurance is regularly sold, and prices are set competitively. In the Pacific, established markets are those that are regulated and have multiple insurance companies and/or market players operating within the country.
External shocks	Unexpected events that originate due to reasons outside the control of a country which may have a significant impact on the country. For example, natural hazards, health emergencies, and global economic crises.
Indemnity insurance	Type of insurance contract that insures a policyholder against losses to specific assets (and sometimes against the financial consequences of these losses), subject to proof of loss and adequacy of the sums insured.
Infrastructure	Physical and organizational structure and facilities required for the operation of a society or enterprise.[3] Categories include but are not limited to agriculture, natural resources, rural development, human and social development, transport, energy, urban development, and water.

---

[1]   S. Taylor. 2023. Contract Works Insurance. https://getindemnity.co.uk/business-insurance/contract-works-insurance

[2]   Cambridge Dictionary. 2023. Cambridge University Press & Assessment 2023. https://dictionary.cambridge.org/dictionary/english/contractor.

[3]   Cambridge Dictionary. 2023. Cambridge University Press & Assessment 2023. https://dictionary.cambridge.org/dictionary/english/infrastructure.

Local participation	Use of workers and materials from the country that an infrastructure project is based in, rather than from another country.
Loss adjuster	Person or firm who assesses the amount of compensation that should be paid to an insurance policyholder after they have made a claim on their insurance policy.
National (re)insurance company, broker, or contractor	This guide uses "national" to refer to any (re)insurance company or broker working within any of the 14 Pacific countries.
Parametric insurance	Type of risk financing instrument that pays out a pre-agreed amount to a policyholder, according to predefined events and/or hazard characteristics (e.g., wind speed). Key advantages of parametric insurance include (i) quick payouts (typically within weeks) that are guaranteed when the predefined hazard thresholds are met, (ii) reduced time and resources needed to communicate the underlying analysis and build trust with policyholders, (iii) more cost-effective pricing (from a market perspective) due to its simplicity and familiarity, and (iv) lean claims process.
Premium	This guide refers to the monetary sum paid by a policyholder to the principle such as the (re)insurer for an insurance policy.
Procurement	This guide uses "procurement" to refer to the methodology and process used to obtain goods, works, and services required for infrastructure projects.
Reinsurers	Insurers who provide insurance protection to other insurance companies (reinsurance). Reinsurance is typically purchased where the accumulated risk written by an insurer is beyond their financial resources (for example disaster or catastrophe risk) and/or the insurer does not have the technical expertise to underwrite the risk. Reinsurance differs from co-insurance as the primary insurer retains full, legal responsibility for payment to the insured, even if 100% of the risk is passed to a reinsurer (known as fronting).
(Re)insurers	Generic term to cover insurers and/or reinsurers.
Risk engineer	Person or firm who identifies, analyzes, and minimizes risks associated with infrastructure projects.
Risk reduction measures	Measures to reduce the chances of damage or losses from a particular hazard. Measures can be in multiple forms, including, but not limited to financial measures (e.g., insurance), structural measures (e.g., building a structure to a building code standard), and educational measures (e.g., implementing a fire safety plan).
Underwriting	Process through which an individual or institution (e.g., an insurance company) evaluates and takes on the financial risk of another party for a fee.
Valuer	Person who estimates the value of infrastructure constructions and associated indirect costs.